John Corbet Anderson

The Roman City of Uriconium at Wroxeter, Salop

John Corbet Anderson

The Roman City of Uriconium at Wroxeter, Salop

ISBN/EAN: 9783742829849

Manufactured in Europe, USA, Canada, Australia, Japa

Cover: Foto ©Thomas Meinert / pixelio.de

Manufactured and distributed by brebook publishing software
(www.brebook.com)

John Corbet Anderson

The Roman City of Uriconium at Wroxeter, Salop

THE

ROMAN CITY

OF

U R I C O N I U M

AT

𝔚roreter, Salop:

ILLUSTRATIVE OF THE HISTORY AND SOCIAL LIFE OF
OUR ROMANO-BRITISH FOREFATHERS.

BY

J. CORBET ANDERSON.

WITH NUMEROUS CUTS,

DRAWN ON WOOD FROM THE ACTUAL OBJECTS, BY THE AUTHOR.

—

LONDON:
J. RUSSELL SMITH, SOHO SQUARE.

—

MDCCCLXVII.

CONTENTS.

· ILLUSTRATIONS.

[1] Viewed from Cressage, as from thence the peculiar conical shape of the back-bone ridge of the Wrekin is seen to greatest advantage. Uriconium was situated at the foot of this mountain, to the left. The shattered trunk of a tree, represented as enclosed in the foreground, is the celebrated Christ's Oak, alluded to in Domesday Book. This tree is a living link between us and the Saxon time.

LIST OF OTHER WOODCUTS.

vi

INTRODUCTION.

OF that dark pre-historic time, the so-called
Celtic age, when vast migrations from remote
quarters of the globe spread themselves over
Northern and Western Europe — of the ages
designated the Stone and Bronze periods — this .
book does not treat. Nor does it refer to that
dim historic era which succeeded the dismem-
berment of the Roman Empire, when, if we
would be correctly informed concerning the
equipment and usages of the Teutonic conquerors
of Europe, we must search their graves.

The following pages relate to a city, built
about the middle of the first century, in our
own country, by soldiery of the Roman Empire.
They called it Uriconium, and a fragment of its

ruins (for the city perished after flourishing about four hundred years), is to be seen at Wroxeter, distant about five miles from Shrewsbury, Salop. The locality was chosen as one calculated to yield a store of antiquities, which might throw fresh light on the Roman occupation of Britain. A well-directed excavation, accordingly, laid bare a portion of the site, and the result was the recovery of a collection of relics, although this was neither so large, or so good, as might have been expected from the area and number of rooms uncovered. The circumstance that the majority of the apartments in question, apparently, had belonged to a system of Roman public baths may in some measure account for the inferior character of most of the things found in them; but the particular situation in which these relics were dug up precludes the possibility of doubting they were Roman.

I am not aware of any particular description of article having been found at Wroxeter but what is common to other Romano-British sites.

Being familiar with the story, and having visited the ruins of Uriconium, and made drawings from the objects dug up there, it occurred to me that an illustrated work on this Romano-British town might prove interesting to those who prefer fact to fiction, especially as the matter relates to a period of the history of our own country, concerning which no very certain knowledge can be obtained from books. The only coeval notices of the Roman domination in Britain are those penned by Tacitus, and one or two other foreigners. These recount how Britain was overrun and subdued by the Roman legions, and how every attempted insurrection of its unfortunate inhabitants was quelled. Yet surely something else besides a military movement is required to make up the life of a nation during four hundred years? Of this internal British existence, however, little or no notice is taken by the authorities alluded to. The truth is, if we would ascertain the nature and degree of the civilisation imparted to Britain by the Romans,

we must seek for it under the soil, and in such
archæological enquiries as those of which Uriconium has been recently the field.

The time is past when works relating to ancient
and historical monuments failed to attract attention ; every year the science of antiquity becomes
more comprehensible and acceptable.

That this little book may tend to spread a love
for, and an intelligent appreciation of, monuments
which evidence the ancient and gradual establishment of institutions we enjoy, is the wish of its
author.

URICONIUM.

CHAPTER I.

THE SITE.

A LITTLE to the west of the remarkable Shropshire mountain the Wrekin, which, rearing from a vast plain its solitary crest upwards to an altitude of thirteen hundred and twenty feet, is visible from various points of a radius of sixty miles round, the Roman conquerors built the city of Uriconium. The Celtic Dre or Wre, Wre, signifies a *hill* high or *rotund*. The Romans Latinized Wre into Uri, for it is most likely that this station of theirs derived its name from the very conspicuous natural landmark near it. The terminative *conium* seems to be a Latinized edition of the Celtic *cond*, signifying an embouchure, which also agrees with the situation of Uriconium.

The contemplation of the remains of this Roman city is fraught with interest to every student of the ancient history of our country. Uriconium owed its foundation, it is conjectured, to the campaigns of Ostorius, about A.D. 50. A British

B

town may previously have occupied the site, but as yet there is no positive evidence to that effect. Planted on the north, or north-eastern side of the Severn, not far from where the Tern empties itself into that river, the Uriconium of Roman times appears to have been a large town encircled by a vallum and fosse.

The dark line A A A in the accompanying map (*see plate* I.), will give the reader an idea of the irregular oval-like shape of the vallum, or wall, that enclosed within its circuit the Romano-British city. Hartshorne estimated this vallum to have once been fifteen feet in height, but a recent excavation, made where it is most prominent, showed it to be raised only nine feet above the bottom of the ditch; the fosso was found to be ninety-five feet wide. Examined at various points, it has been ascertained that this wall is formed merely of a bank of rubble, faced outwardly with a mass of clay, or of small stone boulders, set in clay. The singular form, as well as the extent of the line of circumvallation of Uriconium, tend to prove that, originally an open town, Uriconium did not become a walled city until a late period; probably the period of intestine warfare which preceded the separation of this province from the empire. The wall that surrounded Uriconium is rather more than three miles in circumference. The plough has long since passed over its surface,

Plate I.

THE SITE OF URICONIUM AT WROXETER, SALOP

yet the mound which covers its remains can still be traced; that portion of it bounding the city on its south-eastern extremity forming, indeed, a bold projection.

The land upon which the Roman city was built rises precipitously at first from the river Severn on the south-west, until it gradually reaches its highest elevation at B. From B the ground then sinks towards the Bell Brook; on the other side of which it again rises towards the north. Uriconium, therefore, stood upon two hillocks, separated by a valley, at the bottom of which coursed a streamlet.

Upon its eastern side the city was approached by the famous Roman road, the Watling Street; it penetrated the city wall at C, at which point the gate was guarded, probably, by some defensive works; and thus this distant station was connected with London, Rutupiæ or Richborough in Kent, and the continent. Between those important Roman towns on the South Welsh border, *Blestium*, Monmouth, *Magnæ*, Kenchester, and *Bravinium*, the exact site of which remains undetermined, another highway communicated. This *via*, also called Watling Street, crossed the river Onney at Stretford Bridge, and thence passing by Church Stretton, namely Scrœc Tun—Town of the Street—so called in allusion to the Roman road, this eventually crossed the Severn, and reached

the southern extremity of Uriconium; but the
exact point at which it entered is uncertain. The
dotted line in the Ordnance Map, intended to
represent the course of the city wall at its southern point, the reader will observe assumes a
peculiar shape at D. It is, moreover, a dotted
line, as if a conjectural one. In an old and apparently carefully executed map of this site, the
form of the city wall is given, as indicated by the
dotted lines marked E in our plan, which describe
a fortified entrance not uncommon to strongholds
of Roman construction.[1] It is possible that the
Watling Street which came from the south-west,
crossed the Severn considerably to the south of the
existing ancient paved ford at F by a bridge, and
entered Uriconium at the point E. It is certain
the Roman road alluded to entered Uriconium
somewhere at its southern extremity.

A third great Roman road pierced the city wall
on its north-western side, probably near where it
crosses the Bell Brook; since appearances are in
favour of the supposition that the present road,
which goes by way of Tern Bridge and Atcham
to Shrewsbury, runs upon the line of the old

---

[1] See plan of walls of Roman station at Richborough, MR. C.
ROACH SMITH's work on the *Antiquities of Richborough, Reculver, and Lymne*, p. 44. A similar defensive arrangement may be
seen in the plan of Roman walls of Carcassonne, p. 17 of *Essay
on the Military Architecture of the Middle Ages*, by E. VIOLLET-
LE-DUC. Translation published by J. H. and J. Parker, 1860.

5

Roman road that communicated with *Segontium*, near Caernarvon, and *Deva*, or Chester.

By means of such variously divergent lines, the Romans maintained an easy communication between the most distant limits of the empire and this, their settlement upon the Welsh border. The importance of these great connecting highways, in a military point of view, will readily be comprehended. Uriconium, indeed, occupied a position which, protected on the west and on the north by the rivers Severn and Tern, was capable of offering a strong defence against an assailant.

Yet, not only in a military sense was the city well planted, the site it occupies is one of eminent beauty. Beneath the Roman city the broad and majestic Severn flows onwards towards the ocean. Not more than four miles due eastward the Wrekin rears its vast wooded crest. In the extreme south the lofty Brown Clee Hill peeps above the highest land. A little further to the right the Lawley and Caradoc shoot their sharp purple peaks abruptly into the sky, forming very conspicuous objects in the landscape. More westwardly range the Stretton Hills, and the bold Breidden; whilst beyond are visible in the remote distance the lofty mountains of Wales. Combined, these form a lovely panorama. With the exception of Haughmond Hill, the country to the north is comparatively flat, yet it is a fertile plain; indeed, the soil generally in the neighbourhood of the ancieut Roman city is good.

Viroconium, Οὐιροκόνιον, is mentioned by Ptolemy, the Alexandrian geographer, who wrote about the year A.D. 120; from whence it is certain that this city was existent in the early part of the second century. We learn from Ptolemy, also, that it was situated in the country of the Cornavii.[1] Uroconium, Viroconium, are named respectively in the second and twelfth Itineraries of Antoninus, supposed to have been composed about the year A.D. 320; in the former of these the town is described as occupying a position almost mid-way between the Roman station Rutunio, *Rowton*, and Uxacona, *Oaken-Gates*, both of which are in Shropshire. Richard of Cirencester alludes to this Romano-British city in his first, second, and thirteenth Iter. Finally, Uriconium is mentioned in the treatise compiled by the anonymous geographer of Ravenna. Naming in his chronicle the principal towns of the Carnabii, Richard of Cirencester adds, "and the mother of the rest, Uriconium, esteemed one of the largest cities in

---

[1] The British tribe of the Cornavii, Carnavii or Carnabii, inhabited the district now occupied by the counties of Warwickshire, Worcestershire, Shropshire, Staffordshire, and Cheshire. To the north-east of the Cornavii dwelt the great tribe of the Brigantes. The celebrated Silures peopled Herefordshire and the country to the south-west.

THE WREKIN.

Uriconium was situated at the foot of this Mountain to the left

SITE OF URICONIUM.

Caer Caradoc in mid-distance.

Britain."[1] Richard, however, is not considered
a first-rate authority; yet, be this as it may,
beyond his brief allusion to it, and the bare men-
tion of its name as previously stated, history is
silent respecting this undoubtedly once great
Romano-British town.

Leland observes, "the destruction of *Roxceter*
by all likelyhood was the cause of the erection of
Shrewsbury,"[2] but he makes no comment on the
appearance of the site in his day. Camden, who
visited the spot about forty years afterwards, and
the first edition of whose *Britannia* was published
in 1586, writes, "I saw nothing here besides a
few pieces of walls (commonly called the *old work
of Wroxceter*), built of hewn stone, divided by
seven rows of British brick and arched on the
inside:"[3] it is the old wall to which Camden
refers.

---

[1] *Chron. Rich. of Cirencester*, B. I., ch. 6.
[2] LELAND'S *Itinerary*, by Hearne, vol. iv., pt. 2nd, fol. 181 h.
[3] CAMDEN'S *Britannia*, by Gough, vol. ii, p. 397.

CHAPTER II.

FORMER DISCOVERIES.

THAT the Roman town of Uriconium was destroyed by some great conflagration was proved during the course of the late excavations by the abundant traces of burning found. It is the local tradition, also, that the city was destroyed by fire, and the land comprised within the circuit of its walls, when stirred by the plough or spade, is distinguished from that without the walls by a remarkably black appearance, caused apparently by a mixture of burnt materials. The earth is particularly black on the sloping banks of the Bell Brook, the lower parts of the site, where may have been built of wood the houses of the poorer inhabitants of the Romano-British town.

The village of Wroxeter occupies the southern extremity of the site of Uriconium. The Norman scribe spelt the name in Domesday Book Rochescestre, of which the terminating *cestre* plainly is derived from the Latin *castra*, signifying a camp or fortified place. In a document of the year 1350 the name is spelt Wroxcestre, from whence the transition to the modern Wroxeter is easy.

William the Conqueror's commissioners have

described Rochescestre merely as a manor, peopled
by a few inhabitants, from whence it may
be inferred that, when Domesday Book was
written 800 years ago, the city had long been
numbered with the dead. The varied evidences
which it supplies of the progress of art and civili-
zation in this distant province of the Roman
empire—this once extensive settlement of that
wonderful race upon the border of Wales—had
been overlooked and forgotten amid the confusion
and barbarism of the succeeding times. In silence
profound as the grave deep lay the charred and
blackened ruins of Uriconium beneath the accumulation of ages. For the rain and snow decom-
posing the mass of burnt material, the summer
sun would soon cause a rank vegetation to spring
up, which again annually decaying, in the course
of centuries a vast deposit gathered over the surface of the floors. Roman walls, however, are
far too strongly built to fall down of themselves,
these, therefore, must still have remained projecting above ground, peeping through thickets that
had overgrown them; their nookeries affording,
moreover, an excellent haunt for wild beasts.

Doubtless the desolate spot was shunned by
the Saxon population, whose superstitious minds
would readily clothe the site with every description of imaginable terror. We may estimate the
amount of superstitious dread that pervaded

society during the dark ages, with regard to the
deserted buildings of the previous lords of the
soil, from the circumstance that "all the Bene-
dictionals of the Anglo-Saxon period contain
forms for blessing the vessels of metal or earthenware found in ancient sites, and relieving them
from the spells which had been cast upon them
by the 'Pagans,' in order that the finders might be
enabled to make use of these vessels without any
personal danger." It is a fact that, during these
benighted times, when people found any of the
bronze figures or inscribed stones, so common to
Roman sites, they were under the greatest appre-
hension of personal danger until they had mutilated them, so as to counteract, as they believed,
the charms of the old magicians. Having mutilated them, they then flung them into the nearest
river.

It will be readily understood, therefore, how it
came to pass that the ugly, blackened ruins of
Uriconium remained untouched for centuries. In
forlorn condition, what remained above-ground of
the Roman city at length came into the hands of
the Normans, when the Church, having broken
the spell that hovered over the mysterious spot,
the mediæval builders took to pillaging the site
for building materials, of which, doubtless, they
found an immense supply ready to hand. The
walls of the churches of Wroxeter and Atcham,

and those of Haughmond Abbey, exhibit tiles
and stones certainly furnished from the ruins of
the Roman city. The old town, there is reason
to believe, was also one of the principal quarries
whence were derived the materials employed in
the erection of many other structures, lay as well
as ecclesiastical, now standing, for miles around
Wroxeter.

The mediæval builders having in the course of
time used up the materials supplied by the extensive ruins of Uriconium, and reduced its walls to
the level of the ground, that is, to the level of
the ground as it existed in their day, it does not
appear that they dug below the surface for more
material, but they seem to have left the place
alone, and so a fresh accumulation was permitted
to gather over the site. This will account for the
appearances presented during the late excavations.
Two or three feet below the present surface of the
soil the excavators found the tops of the walls as
the mediæval builders had left them, with fragments of plaster, and broken tiles and stones,
which they had not thought it worth while to
carry away. The walls were then found perfect
for five or six feet further down, at which depth
the excavators came upon the ground-floor of the
Roman houses. These floors, therefore, were in
all some eight or nine feet below the ordinary
level of the land.

Ever since the city was destroyed it has probably been the popular belief that hidden treasures lie buried beneath its ruins. We learn from an old MS. chronicle[1] of the monks of Worcester, that in the year 1287, at a place by Wroxeter, called "Bilebury," the fiend was compelled by an enchanter to appear to a certain lad, and show him where lay buried "urns, and a ship, and a house, with an immense quantity of gold." Another record, of the close of the thirteenth century, informs us how certain treasure-hunters at Wroxeter, caught in the act, were brought before the court of the lord of the manor, to whom belonged the right of treasure-trove, and only escaped a feudal dungeon because, as luck would have it, they did not find the treasure for which they had dug.[1] These notices suffice to indicate that the Salopians of former times were fully alive to the notion, that something worth searching for lay buried underground hereabouts. That from time immemorial coins, or *dinders*,[3] as the peasantry call them, and other articles of the Roman period, have been ploughed up on various parts of the site of Uriconium, and carried away, is certain ; and it is not unlikely

---

[1] Printed in WARTON'S *Anglia Sacra*.
[2] See EYTON'S *Antiquities of Shropshire*, vol. vii. p. 310, *note*.
[3] A name doubtless derived from the Anglo-Norman *denier*, which again represents the Latin *denarius*.

that systematic searches even have been made on
the spot for treasure from time to time, although
no record remains to tell us of the proceedings.
Approaching nearer to our own day, we learn
that in 1701 a hypocaust was uncovered, " walled
about and floored, under and over," with a tessellated pavement in good preservation ; they were
found in the field at the spot marked B in our
plan.[1] A square tesselated pavement was found
in 1706. It would appear that one of the hypocausts recently excavated had been uncovered in
the early part of the last century, for Baxter,
whose *Antiquitates Britannicæ* was published in
1733, founds upon this circumstance his opinion,
that the building to which the "old wall" belonged was a bath. Mr. Dukes, in his manuscript,[2] gives a drawing of a tesselated floor found
at Wroxeter in 1734 ; the form is oblong, and
semicircular at one extremity ; it is composed of
green, red, white, and blue tesseræ, the green
forming the outside border. In 1747, a paper
was read before the Royal Society relative to a
quantity of clay moulds for forging Roman coins
that were found at Wroxeter. These had on
them the head of Julia, the wife of Severus, and
the inscription, JVLIA AVGVSTA. In 1752,

---

[1] Described in vol. xxv. of the *Philosophical Transactions.*
[2] Mr. DUKES' MS., *Illustrated Account of Wroxeter*, in possession of Society of Antiquaries of London.

14

three sepulchral stones, having Latin inscriptions
on them, were found in a field about two hundred
yards north-east of the old wall.[1]

In 1788, at the spot indicated by the letter G
in our little map, there was a grand discovery of
Roman remains made.[2] These consisted of coins,
both of the Upper and Lower Empire; bones of
animals, some of which were burnt; fragments
of earthen vessels, of various sizes and shapes;
pieces of glass; a piece of leaden pipe, not sol-
dered, but hammered together, and the seam or
juncture secured by a kind of mortar; tessellated
floors of rooms; baths, and hypocausts. In one
of the latter pieces of painted stucco were found,
some striped crimson on a yellow ground; others
intersecting chequer-work of one colour, red or
blue.

The following notice of a discovery, made
Feb. 8th, 1798, is preserved in Mr. Parkes'
manuscripts in the British Museum[3]:—"Between
Tern Bridge and the Severn, at Attingham, in a
ploughed field, at a little more than plough depth,
an enclosure of large stones was come upon,
within which were ranged three large glass urns,

[1] Engraved in *Camden*, vol. iii. p. 13. The originals are preserved in the library of Shrewsbury Grammar School.
[2] Described in a communication made in the following year
to the Society of Antiquaries by the Rev. FRANCIS LEIGHTON,
and printed in the *Archæologia*, vol. ix.
[3] MS. addit., No. 21,011, p. 37.

of very elegant workmanship, one large earthen urn, and two small ones, of fine red earth. Each of the urns had one handle, and the handles of the glass urns were elegantly ribbed. The glass urns were twelve inches high, by ten in diameter. The large earthen urn was so much broken that the size could not be ascertained; on the handle were the letters SPAII. The small urns are about nine inches high. With the *glass urns* were *burnt bones* and fine mould, and in each a fine glass lachrymatory of the *same* material; these had a most beautiful light green tint. Near one of them was part of a jaw-bone, an earthen lamp, and a few Roman coins of the Lower Empire, of little value. The whole were covered with large flat stones, covered with a quantity of coarse rock-stone." As noticed in the manuscript, this was probably the burial-place of some family of Uriconium.

A very curious relic was found at Wroxeter, whilst ploughing near the old wall in 1808, namely, a small stamp, such as were used by Roman empirics and *ocularii*. It is formed of fine-grained green schist; is of the exact size, and in-scribed as represented in the annexed cut. The abbreviated Latin in-

scription may be extended as follows:—TI*Berii*
CL*audii Medici* DIALIB*Anum* AD OMNE
VIT*ium Oculorum* EX O*co*, which, rendered into
English, signifies "the *dialibanum* (collyrium or
salve) of Tiberius Claudius, the physician, for all
complaints of the eyes, to be used with egg."[1]

Several urns were found here in the year 1810,
and a quantity of silver coins, in a glass vessel
with two handles.

In 1827, a handsome tesselated pavement was
discovered in what was then a stack-yard; at II,

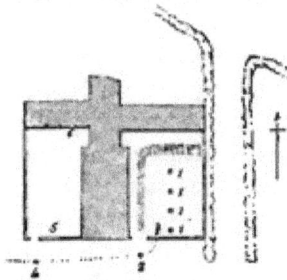

Fig 1

in our map. It was
destroyed, however, by
the folk who rushed
from Shrewsbury to
see it, before a draw-
ing could be made.

When the late Mr.
Stanier was clearing
the ground for the
foundations of the farm
buildings that stand by
the side of the Watling
Street Road at I (*see
map*), in the year
1855, he found, in
what is now the farm-

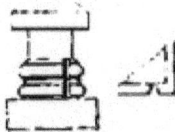

Fig 2

---

[1] This stamp is now in the museum at Shrewsbury.

yard, a row of four short square pillars, marked
1 1 1 1 in the annexed little ground plan. These
pillars stood at equal distances of about ten feet
from each other, and had apparently formed the
front of some building that looked upon the
principal street. The peculiar elevation of these
pillars is represented in fig. 2. Each had a ver-
tical groove on the sides of its base facing the
adjoining pillars, as if formed to hold some connecting work, wooden or otherwise, which had
once extended from pillar to pillar. A fifth pillar
was found out of the line of the others, at 2,
fig. 1; and a large squared stone at 3. In laying
the drain, indicated by the dotted line, a concrete
floor was found five feet below the surface, and
there were scattered about a number of large
stones, iron cramps, bones, lead, etc., among which
a silver coin was picked up. A flag-stone was
discovered at 4; at 5, a floor of flag-stones was
met at a depth of six feet. Digging for the
foundation, at 6, they came upon a gold coin;
but this is said to have been carried away, and
sold privately, by the man who found it.

It is reported that buildings were found under
the smith's shop, situated by the roadside at J (*see
map*); it is even said that the smith's anvil has for
its foundation a large capital of a Roman column.

Scattered over the whole site, indeed, are known
to exist remains of structures; and as the crops

c

of corn approach maturity in the fields enclosed
within the line of circumvallation, the foundations, apparently of rows of houses, are indicated
by the advanced ripeness of the grain growing
over their walls. Roman buildings exist under
the lawn of the vicarage adjoining Wroxeter
Church. At K there is a knoll, which, opened,
was found to be full of the remains of some
building; it might have been a Roman tower
that had formerly commanded the ford, or these
may mark the spot where frowned the mediæval
stronghold, said to have been called Arundel
Castle, in honour of the FitzAlans, Earls of
Arundel, the feudal lords of this territory in the
fourteenth century. The large field, marked B
in the plan, has buildings under every part. At
L were found traces of a street. At N, the
excavators cleared out and exposed to view a
capitally built, ancient, circular stone well; some
doubt, however, whether it be Roman.

Yet while all else lay buried, a solitary fragment of Uriconium, remaining high above ground,
indicated where once a Roman station flourished.
Standing in a field to his left, this huge piece of
masonry has for ages attracted the attention of
the traveller, as he journeyed by the high road
from Buildwas to Shrewsbury. Long known as
the "Old Wall," it is a very interesting monument of the past.

THE OLD WALL.

CHAPTER III.

LATE EXPLORATION.

WE now proceed to lay before the reader the result of those explorations that were lately made upon the site of Uriconium. The old wall, alluded to in the previous chapter, stands on high ground, nearly in the centre of the ancient city, the vast fragment measuring seventy-two feet in length, by upwards of twenty feet in height. Commencing their labours on the 3rd of February, 1859, upon its northern side, the excavators did not find the bottom of this old wall until they had dug into the ground a depth of fourteen feet; the last ten of which, sunk in the natural substratum of sand, proved that this wall had a very deep foundation. They soon discovered that the wall alluded to was continued underground to the west, whilst excavations made in a northerly direction revealed the lower portions of three other enormous walls, running in a direction almost parallel with the old wall. Persevering through many months—in short, spite of various interruptions, until the last month of the year 1862—at length two out of the four acres, kindly placed at the disposal of the Excavation Committee

by the late Duke of Cleveland, owner of the site,
having been explored, under the able direction of
Mr. Thomas Wright, the well-known antiquary,
upon these two acres were found buildings, the
situation of which is indicated by the letter M in
plate I., and a ground plan given in *plate* V.

A A A, *plate* V., represent an extensive square,
enclosing what are supposed to be the remains of
the public Baths of the city.

B B. The "old wall."

C C C C C. Five rooms, the division walls and
also vaulting of the barrel roofs of three of which
can be distinctly traced on the southern face of
the old wall (*see plate* VI.). The most easterly of
these rooms has had its interior walls ornamented,
not with fresco painting, as usually was the case,
but with tesselated work, a fragment of the lower
edge of which, consisting of a guilloche border,

still remains on the
southern wall. The
annexed woodcut
represents this in-
teresting example
of wall tesselation,
which is formed of
red, white, and blu-
ish-grey tesselæ, less
than an inch square. Below, the floor consists
of a plain pavement of cream-coloured tesselæ.

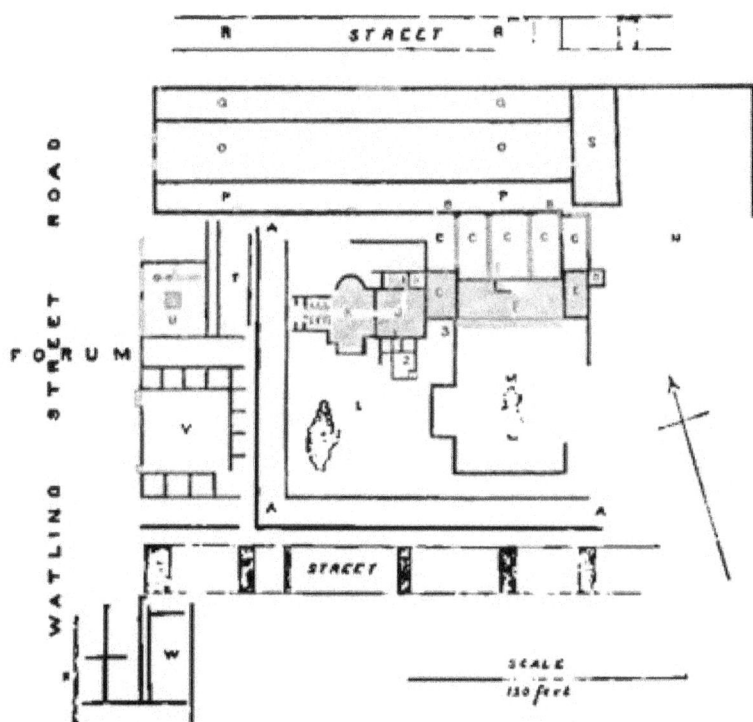

PLAN OF BUILDINGS UNCOVERED ON THE SITE OF URICONIUM.

Apparently, this room had been a Bath. Remains of tesselated work on the wall were also found, in the most westerly of these five apartments. Of the remaining three rooms, the first one to the left appears, from a quantity of burnt wheat found in it, to have been a storehouse for grain. To the south of the central room is a square pit, or cesspool, across the bottom of which a drain runs nearly north and south. The channel of this drain is formed of large roof-tiles, the flanged edges being turned up, so as to form the sides. This drain runs through a well constructed oblong square opening in the wall, that separates C from F.

D. A small chamber, eight feet square, with red brick or tile pavement, arranged in zigzag or herring-bone pattern. The subjoined was sketched from the pavement alluded to, the bricks of which are 4½ inches long by 1 inch wide, and about 2½ inches deep.

On the western side of D a wide opening communicates with E, a hypocaust, but all that remained of many of its columns were their bases.

The Romans did not warm their rooms by fires kindled in fireplaces as we do. They adopted a

totally different method to obtain the requisite amount of heat. To warm the superior apartments they sent hot air under their floors. The floors, formed of cement, generally eight or ten inches thick, consequently required to be supported upon rows of short pillars; the hot air coursed through these rows of underneath pillars, and this arrangement was termed the hypocaust, from a Greek word signifying *fire* or *heat underneath*. Running up the northern wall of the apartment E are the impressions of lines of flue tiles, hardly an inch apart, from whence it may be inferred that this particular room was intended to have been much heated. It was a *sudatarium* or sweating-room probably. The flue tiles had been cramped to the walls by iron crumps. Two skeletons were found in this hypocaust, one of which was that of a young person.

F. Large hypocaust, upon the northern wall of which an inscription, scrawled by some pointed instrument in large straggling characters, was found; but before it could be examined two casual visitors amused themselves by breaking with the ends of their walking-sticks the plaster upon which the Latin lines were written, and thus what may have been a deeply interesting record was wantonly destroyed.

G. Another hypocaust. In this one three skeletons were found; one being that of a female, another that of a very old man, found in a crouching position in the north-west corner of the hypocaust. Near the old skeleton lay a heap of coins, 132 in number. Scattered among the coins were a number of small iron nails, and traces of the decomposed wood of the little box, or coffer, that had contained them. It has been conjectured that the persons of whom these were the skeletons, a helpless old man, probably, and two women, had crept into this hypocaust through the aperture in which the fire had been kindled in its southern wall, to avoid the massacre which is supposed to have preceded the burning of the city by the barbarians. If so, the unhappy fugitives, after creeping on their hands and knees under the floor of the room to the furthest corner of the hypocaust, had in this place been stifled by the remains of hot air from the firing that warmed the houses, or destroyed by the conflagration of the latter.

II. A small room, with red brick pavement of herring-bone pattern; a similar apartment to the one marked D.

I. Here is a massive stair of three steps, formed of large stones; when this staircase was first uncovered it was blocked up by the shaft of a column that lay across it, as if fallen from above. A corner, at the bottom of the steps, seems to have been a common receptacle for dust, etc.,

swept from floors and passages, as the earth, for
eighteen inches in depth hereabouts, was filled with
bone needles, hair pins, fibulæ or brooches, broken
pottery, glass, coins, nails, and various articles in
iron, bronze, and lead; bones of birds and animals that had been eaten, stags' horns, tusks and
hoofs of wild boars, oyster shells, in one of which
lay the shell of a large nut, etc. This outside
stair with the three steps led downwards towards
an arched passage, where, probably, the fire had
been kindled, the hot air from which was blown
into the hypocaust

J, into which this passage runs. The bricks,
forming the sides of the passage alluded to, are
much cracked and blackened by the action of fire.
Between J, and

K, another and larger hypocaust; there is a
communication through the partition wall. This
latter hypocaust appears to have supported, on at
least one hundred and twenty columns, formed of
square flat bricks piled up to the height of about
three feet, the floor of a handsome room, measuring thirty-five feet by fifty, inclusive of the semi-
circular northern end. A small portion of the
floor remained at the north-eastern corner. It
was a mass of concrete eight inches thick, the
upper surface of which had formed a plain smooth
floor. A complicated arrangement of walls, and
a quantity of unburnt coal, were found on the

ROMAN BUILDINGS UNCOVERED ON THE SITE OF URICONIUM.

ROMAN BUILDINGS UNCOVERED ON THE SITE OF URICONIUM.

western side of this hypocaust, apparently connected with the heating of it. Its massive
northern wall was plastered and painted both
externally and internally, the exterior of the
semi-circular end being painted red, with stripes
of yellow. The exposure to the air, after having
been buried so many ages, has caused, however,
both plaster and paint to crumble away into
dust. Near this northern wall lay an immense
stone, evidently shaped so as to form part of a
huge stone band, intended to fit its semi-circular
end. The huge stone is now placed on the top of
the semi-circular wall, which it fits exactly. To
the stone is attached a strong piece of iron, sol-
dered into it with lead. The skull and some of the
bones of a young child were found in what appears
to have been a court-yard, outside the semi-circular
end of this hypocaust, as if the infant had been
slain and thrown out.

It is hypocaust K, with its remaining pillars,
that is represented in the foreground of *plate* VI.[1]

---

[1] When hypocaust K was first uncovered one hundred and
twenty pillars were counted standing in it, but these were shortly
afterwards ruthlessly overthrown by a party who came to inspect
the ruins of the Roman city. The visitors expecting to see more
than met their view, declared the whole affair "a sell"; when,
arrived at this hypocaust, Bill and Jack, to make up for their
disappointment, amused themselves, Englishmen-like, by shying
at its interesting group of pillars, until every one of these were
laid low. Even the piece of floor at the north-eastern corner
was broken down with the rest. From drawings of the hypocaust, made when it was first discovered, Dr. Johnson carefully
rebuilt as many of the columns as he could find unbroken bricks
for the purpose, and restored the bit of floor.

I, Apparently a large irregularly shaped open court. The floor was formed of cement, but at the point indicated there was found what seemed to have been a reservoir, or cold water bath, about three feet in depth, the bottom of which was formed of large flag-stones. A great mound of earth now prevents this from being seen.

On the northern side of L the foundation walls of several small rooms, or offices, have been exposed; the ground hereabouts, however, has not yet been thoroughly explored. Just where fig. 2 is placed the excavators came upon a mass of iron that must weigh at least 1½ cwt. The lump, wrought into a square shape at one end, seems to have been subjected to intense heat; it lays thrown down, between two fragments of sculptured sandstone, as when found. The exit from room 2 into the adjoining interior court is at the south-east corner; the passage is formed of two large square blocks of stone. The wall on the right of the court, into which this passage leads, appears to have been undergoing repair at the moment when Uriconium was surprised, for a large breach in it is filled up with inferior masonry; two large dark unfinished coping stones lie on the ground near; the Roman masons had lifted a third stone on to the top of the wall.

M. An extensive building with cement floor, towards the centre of which, at the depth of about three feet below the floor, was found another pavement, ten feet wide by thirty long, neatly formed with large flat tiles. This, also, probably had been a water tank, or perhaps a Bath. It is now covered over with the debris of the excavations.

A A A appear to have formed a cloister, about thirteen feet wide, running round the western and southern sides of the Baths, the ambulatory, in fact, which the Romans considered a very important adjunct to their Baths. As no traces of buildings could be discovered on the ground N, here, may have been gardens, also usually attached to the public Baths of the Romans.

That the series of buildings we have just described were the public Baths of Uriconium is the opinion entertained by our best antiquaries. Water can be procured, it is said, on the higher ground marked B in the map of site, *plate* I., from whence it probably was conveyed to the reservoir in the baths by leaden pipes, as portions of these were found in digging in the field next the excavations, between M and B, *plate* I. The well formed drain, described as running under the northern wall of F, *plate* V., goes in a northern direction; perhaps it carried the refuse waters of the Baths downwards to the Bell Brook.

As the Baths and the Basilica are alluded to

in Roman inscriptions thus, BALNEVM CVM
BASILICA, as if they were sometimes joined
together, the range of large buildings to the
north of the Baths is conjectured to have been
the Basilica of Uriconium, of which

O O was an enclosure, which, from the openings
and plinths of stone that were found, appears to
have had a grand entrance from the Watling Street
on the west. Supposed to have been an uncovered
one, this court is two hundred and twenty-six feet
long by thirty feet wide, and is paved in its whole
extent with small bricks three inches long by one
inch broad, arranged herring-bone-wise. Fragments of the bases, shafts, and capitals of columns
were scattered about in different parts of this
area. Among other objects found here were two
or three links of a strong iron chain, the steel
head of an axe, and a small iron trident,
originally placed, perhaps, on a staff, as an ensign
of office. To the south of the great court just
described there appears to have been a long open
alley,

P P, the great wall which separates the two,
being four feet in thickness. The northern face
of the "old wall" forms part of the southern
boundary of this alley; it looks like an exterior
one; and this had evidently been the case with
its continuation westward, in which were found
two openings for doors, each approached from the

narrow passage P P by one large squared stone.
The most westerly of these steps, worn down by
people's feet, indicated that this passage had
formerly been much frequented. Originally,
probably, another doorway stood in the "old
wall" itself, but the large ornamental stones
which formed it having been torn away, caused
the gap now remaining (*see plate* IV.).

It is worthy of note that on looking up under
the great breach an impression in the plaster can
be discerned, as if caused by some very large
stone; beneath the breach, on the original level
of the ground, the excavators found a large
capital of a column with plain bands, lying up-
side down, as if it had fallen from above. In
Q Q, the corresponding long range to the
north, in the eastern half of the corridor, were
found pavements of fine mosaic, too fine to be
exposed to the air, so that this particular building
must have formerly been enclosed, and contained,
probably more than one room. About the middle
of the northernmost wall there is a wide breach,
where stood, perhaps, at one time, a fine entrance
from the neighbouring street, R R; the wide
breach in this wall, as in others at Uriconium,
in all probability being caused by the anxiety of
the mediæval builders to obtain the large stones
that formed the handsome doorways.

The width of the range marked P P is uni-

formly fourteen feet; that of the range Q Q is
fourteen feet at its western end, and sixteen at
its eastern; so that the walls of Q Q are not
exactly parallel. No doorway was found to communicate between P P and O O, or between O O
and Q Q, yet, as the walls of separation were in
several places entirely broken away to the foundations, there may have been doors in these
breaches.

Trenches dug northwardly from the outer wall
of Q Q brought to light portions of a continuous
pavement, formed of small round cobble stones,
evidently occupying the middle of a street; the
appearance resembled the street of an old town.
This street, however, and all to the north of the
old wall, has been covered up again, and while
these lines are being written a crop of corn waves
over the presumed Basilica of Uriccnium.

By a reference to the plan, it will be seen that
the buildings we have just been describing stood
at the corner of two streets, which crossed each
other at right angles.

S. An unpaved court-yard, between which and
the great enclosure, O O, a doorway with a step
communicated through the strong partition wall.

T. Public *latrinæ*. Where the letter T is
marked there is a herring-bone pavement of
small bricks, on the left of which a well-con-

structed trench sinks to a depth of eight or ten feet below the level of the central pavement; there is another trench or sewer on the right, but it is narrower, and not so deep.

U. Near the north-western corner of this large and nearly square apartment the excavators found a furnace, or forge, built of red clay, the internal surface of the cavity of which had been completely vitrified by intense heat. As there was much charcoal strewed about, this is supposed to have been the shop of an enameller, or worker in glass or metal. Four or five feet to the east of the furnace stands a remarkable, roughly-formed dark grey stone; it is circular, and has a flat top, as if it had served the purpose of a table for the workman. A huge fragment of the round shaft of a column, also of dark grey stone, lies near; whilst exactly in the centre of the room a pier of masonry, about five feet square, is built. On its western side, the apartment of which we are speaking appears to have been open, or to have had a framework or wide doors of wood, as two great stones lie here with incisions in their sides, made as if to receive a beam.

A very miscellaneous collection of objects was found scattered about in this room: fragments of Samian ware, part of a large bronze fibula, pieces of fine glass, hair-pins, Roman coins; some thirty-eight coins were found together by the entrance

in the western wall. Near lay the remains of a
small earthen vessel, in which the coins had probably been carried by some one who had dropped
them here as he fled from the place.

V. A large quadrangular court, with compartments on the right-hand side, and a row of
chambers on its north and south sides. The open
court which these enclosed appears to have been
paved in its whole extent with small red bricks
or tiles; these are only three inches and three-
quarters long, by seven-eighths of an inch wide.
A large portion of the pavement still remains;
the effect is very good, all crumbled and broken
although the tiles are. What, then, must it have
been when, clean and bright, this pavement was
first laid down by its Roman maker? It is sur-
prising to what an extent their recent exposure
to the air, after having been buried underground
for so many ages, has caused even the hard Roman
bricks and cement to disappear into dust.

In the last chamber to the left in the row to
the north of the court alluded to there was found
a quantity of unused charcoal, as if here had
been a store for that article; along with the
charcoal was found some mineral coal. The
chambers in the northern row were each about
twelve feet square; the one in which the charcoal
was found being no less than ten feet deep, with
a low cross wall at its bottom. In two of the

other chambers, one on the northern and the other on the southern row, were found a quantity of bones of various animals, stags' horns, etc., some of which had been cut and sawn, whilst others had been turned on a lathe; these last-named chambers, therefore, may have been magazines for some bone-worker.

The quadrangular court was approached from the Watling Street on the west by two entrances, one twelve feet wide at its north-west corner; an inclined plane it was, the floor of the court being some three feet above the level of the neighbouring street. The central part of this inclined plane was formed of three great sloping blocks of squared stone, and the rest apparently of smoothed concrete. Some imagine that this wide entrance had been a cartway, and they point to the broken and repaired pavement of the court in confirmation of their opinion : a piece of a horse-shoe is said to have been picked up in this court.

The smaller entrance at the south-west angle was for foot-passengers, the approach from the street being by two massive stone steps, the south-western corners of which are much worn. The passenger traffic coming up the street from the south into this court must have been great indeed to have worn such a hole as there is in the upper step. The hole is two inches deep, and it

D

looks exactly as if one had scooped in the stone the deep imprint of a Roman sandal.

Several weights of different sizes were picked up in court V.; all circumstances considered, therefore, it seems reasonable to conclude that here had been a market, and the surrounding chambers had been shops or depôts of various materials sold by measure.

At the south-eastern corner of V. there is a communication with the lower floor of the gallery that runs in front of the apartments on the eastern side of the court.

Trenches dug in a direction southward of the baths and buildings we have described showed another street running nearly east and west, at right angles with the Watling Street, and parallel with the street north of the Basilica. This admirable arrangement of the streets of Uriconium is laid down in the ground-plan, *plate* V.

W. Remains of a row of houses, which appear to have extended the whole length of the southern side of the adjoining street. A well-made and well-preserved stone gutter, about fifteen inches deep by two feet in width, runs near the western walls of the houses that face the Watling Street at X. At short intervals stones lay in this gutter, in the singular manner here represented; these stones could hardly have fallen accidentally into such a

position. The gutter is now almost covered again with earth.

From the peculiar position of what appeared to have been the front of buildings on the left-hand side of the Watling Street at I, *plate* I., it has been conjectured that the intervening wide space between this supposed line of buildings and the line of buildings to the right of the Watling Street, which we have been describing, was the Forum of Uriconium. If such be the case, then the Basilica held here the same position in regard to the Forum as it does at Pompeii.

Recent excavations revealed the fact that the ancient cemetery of the Roman Uriconium lay without the city wall, extending along either side of the Watling Street.

CHAPTER IV.

ROMAN BUILDINGS.

THE late partial exploration of Uriconium has at least advanced our acquaintance with the manner in which the streets and houses were distributed over the Romano-British towns. The Roman town of Cilurnum at Chesters, in Northumberland, abounds in small alleys. At Durobrivæ, Castor, in Northamptonshire, the houses seem to have been scattered about without any regular order; but the streets that have been uncovered at Uriconium are wide, and they cross each other at right angles. The carriage-ways are paved with small round stones, and there is a pathway for foot-passengers on each side.

That the Romans were first-rate builders, and knew well, not only how to handle bricks and mortar, but how to make both these articles of the best materials that could be obtained, is an undeniable fact; one, moreover, that is confirmed by the ruins of Uriconium.

We have seen that the foundations of the "old wall" had been very securely laid. Reared upon a good foundation, Roman walls have generally one or two set-off courses of stone at the bottom;

upon these are placed a certain number of rows
of facing stones, neatly squared, and then a narrow
string course of bricks, again a number of rows
of facing stones, above which is laid another
bonding course of tiles, and so the rows of stone
and tile courses are repeated until the top of
the wall is reached. The old wall, represented
in *plate* IV., will give the reader an accurate idea
of this particular string-course, characteristic of
Roman masonry.

The Roman builders, however, did not tie
themselves down to follow any uniform rule with
respect to these string-courses, as can be seen in

the annexed cut, representing a portion of two adjoining walls, built at right angles to each other.[1]

[1] The angle marked 3 in *plate* V. is the one represented
above.

38

In the wall to the left, close to the ground, runs a narrow, slightly projecting string-course, composed of a double layer of long flat tiles. Then follow three rows of squared stones, then the string-course of tiles is repeated, then follow four courses of stone, then another double row of tiles, next four more courses of stone, then a fourth bonding course; and, finally, the remains of five rows of stones can be counted ere the broken-off top is reached. On the contrary, fourteen rows of squared stones can be counted in the right-hand wall without the occurrence of a single string-course.

The fragment may serve still further to show how much above a slavish adherence to rule the genius of Roman construction was. Of the four string-courses of tile visible, it is only the upper one that goes through the thickness of the wall; it forms a thorough bonding course; but on the other side of the wall the three lower rows of tiles are not seen.

Like the generality of Roman walls, this left-hand one consists of two proper facings, the interior space between the facings being filled up with rubble mixed with lime. The interior of the wall to the right is also rubble. The side of the wall not seen is, however, formed of very rough masonry; it is evidently the interior side. Material used in wall to the right, light-coloured sandstone; the stone used in wall with the tiles is red sandstone. Both walls are rather over three feet in width; indeed, this appears to have been the average thickness of the walls, partition ones included, of the Roman houses; but frequently in their public buildings, as, for example, in the Basilica of Uriconium, the walls are four feet thick. The walls we have just been describing are not built into, but merely up to each other. It may also be observed that the stones and tiles used in these walls are set in very thick layers of mortar, the marks of the trowel being still visible in several places.

So well did the Romans know how to compound their materials, that the mortar used in the facings of the "old wall" (the portion of Uriconium which has always been exposed above ground) has become as hard as, or even harder than, the stones themselves. The same remark may be applied to that mixture of rubble and lime which composes its interior; plenty of lime has been used, and the mass appears to have been poured in hot. Dr. Collingwood Bruce states, "on the authority of engineers well acquainted with the Roman wall" (Hadrian's *chef-d'œuvre* in the north of England), that the mortar of that structure is precisely similar to the superior prepared grout and concrete which the imperative requirements of modern railway operations have com-

40

pelled the railway mason to adopt. Is it to be
wondered at, then, that the marks of the Roman
trowel are to be seen at Uriconium?

The subjoined represents a small portion of

another wall lately uncovered.[1] Six courses of
red sandstone are first seen above ground, then
three courses of white sandstone are laid upon
them; next follows a string-course of long thin
tiles, above which there remain six more courses
of white sandstone. Now the other side of this
identical wall presents two string-courses of tile;
the one represented, which goes right through
the thickness of the three feet wall, and another
string-course lower down, not appearing on the
side of the wall sketched.

[1] The wall represented in the above cut stands immediately
to the left of the letter T, in plate V.

The Roman red bricks, or tiles rather, are
square and flat. They were not made use of, as
our bricks are, in the construction of the mass of
a wall, but rather in the turning of arches, as
bonding courses, and such-like purposes of strength
and ornament. The application of Roman bricks
to form both a string-course, and likewise the
mouth of a drain, is well illustrated in the foregoing sketch.

The red tiles dug up at Uriconium averaged
seventeen inches in length by twelve inches in
breadth; they were about two inches thick, or
rather less. Some very much larger tiles, however, were found. Fig. 1 represents a flat red tile,

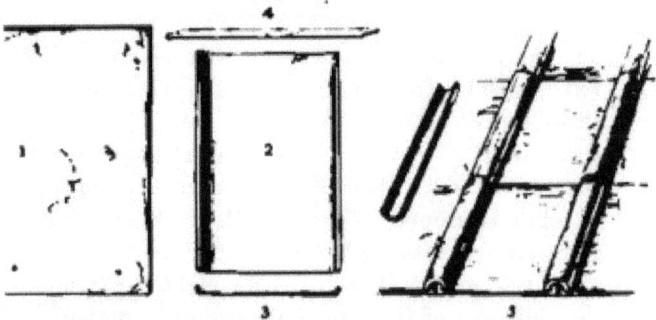

twenty-three inches square; it has a number of
nail holes on its face, and has been set in mortar.
The impress of the foot of an ox is deeply in-
dented on what apparently has been the exposed
surface of this tile. Fig. 2 is a flange edged, red

roofing tile, seventeen inches by eleven and a half, of which fig. 3 is a section, and 4 a side view, to show how the tile is formed to lap into others. The ordinary outside roofing of the Romano-British houses appears to have consisted of large flanged tiles like this; these were supported probably on a strong wooden frame-work. The tiles being laid side by side, a curved tile made on purpose was then placed over their flanges, holding them together in the manner represented in fig. 5, and thus preventing rain from penetrating the interstices.

That many of the buildings at Uriconium had been covered not with tiles, but thick heavy flags, formed of a micaceous laminated sandstone, was apparent from the number of these lying scattered about. The iron nails which had fastened them to the wooden frame-work in many instances remained in their holes. These roof-flags are of

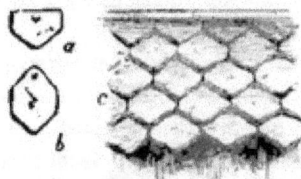

an elongated hexagon shape (b) with a hole at one end for the nail. Half flags (a) were used to form the horizontal top line of the roof. When a number of such as these were in their proper places, they would overlap each other, and present a very pretty lozenge-shaped arrangement on the roof (c).

Slates, such as those now in general use, were not found among the ruins of the Roman city.

As excepting in the case of the fragment known as the "old wall," only the lower portions of the buildings of Uriconium remain, we cannot tell whether or not there were any upper stories to the houses. If we may be allowed to form an opinion from the appearances on the southern face of the old wall, we should incline to suppose they had merely a ground floor, an idea which gains strength as no vestiges of staircases have yet been found in the Roman houses. Nor can it be discovered how the light gained admittance into the houses of Uriconium, as there are no appearances of side windows. It is certain, however, that glazed windows were in use, as fragments of window glass lay strewn about the floors, as if fallen from above; to the edges of some of these pieces mortar still adheres. It seems probable, therefore, that the interior rooms at least had skylights.

We have alluded to the hypocaust system adopted by the Romans to warm their superior apartments, and it has already been noticed how, in order to let the hot air that came from fires kindled in the outer wall course freely under it, the floor of one room at Uriconium rested upon at least one hundred and twenty short columns, whose regularly arranged rows formed in the

aggregate a series of draughty passages. Fig. 1
is a plan of the concrete
formed ground-floor of
the smaller hypocaust,
marked E in *plate* V. The
fire that heated this hypocaust had been kindled in
the outside wall at A. In
all twelve rows of pillars
in depth, and six rows in
breadth, had once stood
in this oblong hypocaust.
The larger sized tile
bases of the pillars were
less than a foot apart, the
pillars themselves being
built of loose tiles eight
inches square and two inches thick. By comparing the remains of these pillars with a photo-
graph of hypocaust K, *plate* V., taken before its
numerous pillars were thrown down, the section,
when perfect, might have been like fig. 2, of which
B represents the ground-floor, and C the floor
supported on the pillars. Hypocaust E, of which
this is a ground-plan and section, be it remembered, is the one that has the remains of flue tiles
running up its side wall, which still stands nine
feet high. Perpendicular flue tiles are shewn at
D D, fig. 2.

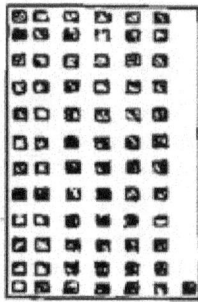

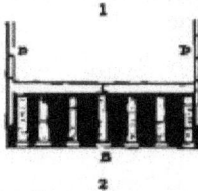

The accompanying is a fragment of a square flue tile found at Uriconium; instead of being striated, or scored, like this one is, some of the flue tiles picked up were striated crossways.

From the description already given of the apartments uncovered at Uriconium, it is evident that the Romans were accustomed to floor or pave their rooms and courts with various materials. Some of the rooms at Uriconium exhibit a plain cement floor, the floors of others are composed of very small bricks, arranged in herring-bone fashion, whilst in the corridor of what is supposed to be the remains of the Basilica were found mosaic pavements. These by no means presented so gorgeous an appearance as some of the tesselated floors that have been found in Britain do, — as that pavement discovered at Leicester, for instance, or the figured floors found in the Roman villas at Woodchester, Cirencester, and Bignor. No pavements have yet been uncovered at Uriconium that can at all compare with these. Nevertheless, the tesselated floors discovered in the Basilica were various in pattern, and all in good taste.

Fragments were distributed throughout the eastern half of the north corridor. There is little doubt that originally the pavement extended the whole length of the corridor, as its western half

hud a concrete foundation, similar to that on
which the fragments found in the eastern half
rested.

Some suppose the space marked P P in *plate V.,*

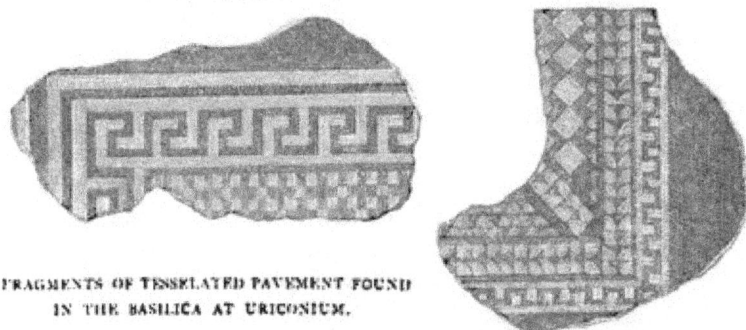

FRAGMENTS OF TESSELATED PAVEMENT FOUND
IN THE BASILICA AT URICONIUM.

like Q Q, was paved throughout with tesselated
mosaic; if so, "two pavements originally existed
at Uriconium very much larger than anything
of the kind previously found in this country."
"Indeed," adds the authority quoted, "on looking
through a large series of records and drawings of
continental tesselated pavements, I cannot find
that any of them equalled in size those at Uriconium."[1] No human figures or animals were
represented on the tesselated fragments found
at Uriconium; the pavement in the corridor

The Pavements of Uriconium, by GEORGE MAW, Esq.,
F.S.A., F.L.S., etc.; read at the Shrewsbury Congress, August
10th, 1860.

consisted of a series of oblong panels, containing a bold arrangement of simple geometrical forms, like the specimens subjoined. Yet, no two panels were exactly similar. The patterns, composed of dark grey and cream-coloured tesselæ, were surrounded, as the generality of Roman pavements are, by a broad field of uniform colour next the wall. This field was of a greenish grey tint.

Composed, as these pavements are, of so many thousand different minute cubes or tesselæ (hardly an inch square), the mere laying of them successfully down itself must have represented an immense amount of skilled labour.

An examination of the foundation upon which these tesselated pavements rested showed this to have been most carefully constructed. It consisted of no less than four distinct layers of materials, forming in the aggregate a substratum nearly three feet in thickness. The uppermost layer, namely, that one in which the tesselæ actually were embedded, consisted of a very hard and white cement, which material was used also in the filling up of the joints. This rested on a perfectly level layer, about 2½ inches thick, composed of a mixture of lime and coarsely powdered burnt earth, or brick rubbish—a cement of extraordinary hardness. Underneath came the third layer, consisting of a bed eight inches thick, of a softer mortar, spread over the lumps of red sandstone that composed the more bulky fourth, or lowermost strata.

The bright tesselæ found at Uriconium are a cream-coloured limestone; the dark bluish tesselæ resemble marble in texture; both, perhaps, were imported. The dark green tesselæ are of a description of stone that occurs at the foot of tho Wrekin. Tesselæ made of red terra-cotta were found in the pavement of the Basilica, and also in that interesting fragment of wall tesselation engraved in p. 20.

It may be added that tho tesselated remains from tho Basilica of Uriconium, preserved in the Shrewsbury Museum, are much discoloured, as if by fire; the effect, probably, of the burning timbers of the building that fell upon tho floors when the city was destroyed.

Nor had the buildings of this Roman town been wanting in architectural decoration, as is apparent from various carved stone fragments found on tho site. In *plate* VII. are represented four fragmentary capitals of columns found at Uriconium. Of these the uppermost one, of an immense size, and scooped out, for many centuries, probably, has done duty as baptismal font in Wroxeter church. On either side of it are sketched the tops of the pillars, into which are fixed the gates in front of this parish church tower. These two

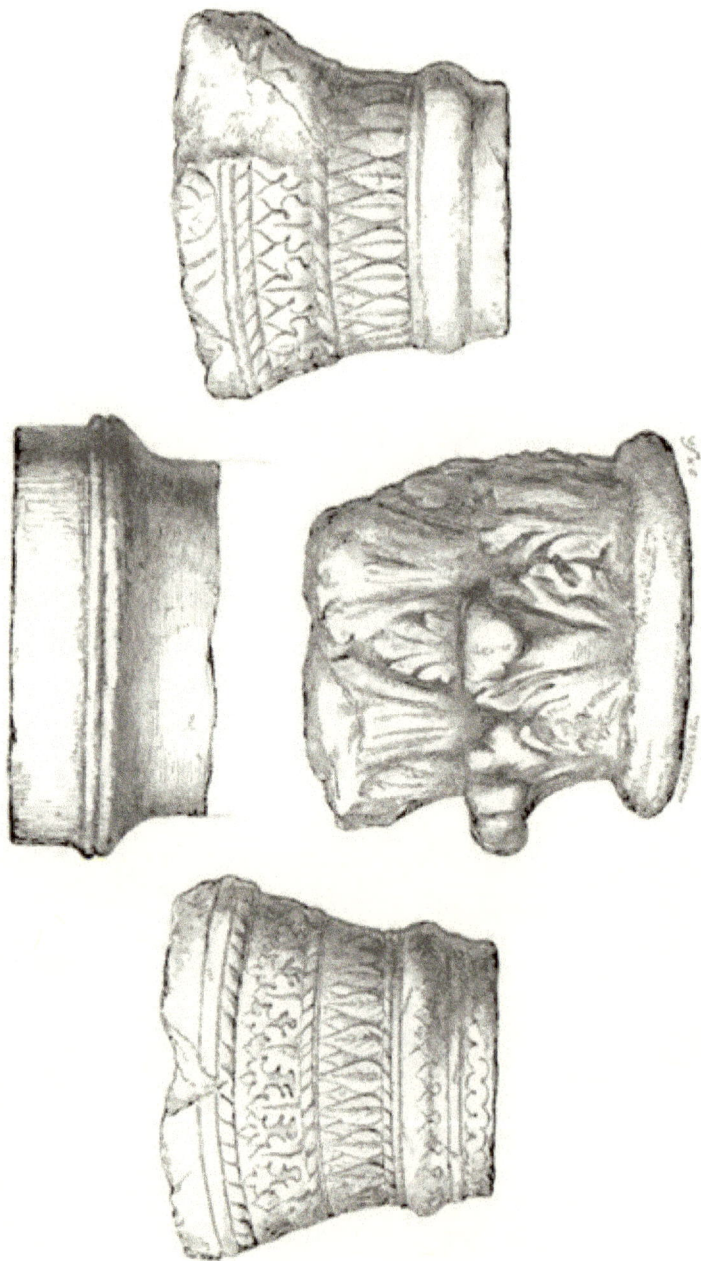

ARCHITECTURAL FRAGMENTS.

Plate VIII.

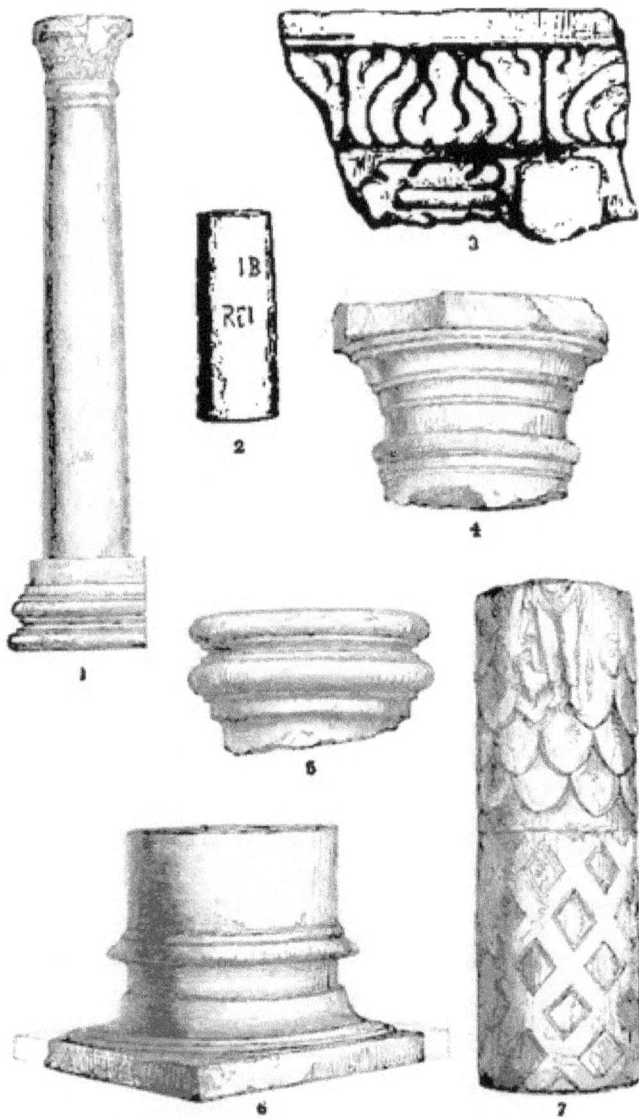

capitals exhibit a rich ornamentation of that late
period of Roman architecture which became the
model of the mediæval Byzantine and Romanesque.
The foliated capital beneath, an enormous fragment, is in the Shrewsbury museum.

A miscellaneous collection of architectural scraps
are clustered together in *plate* VIII. Fig. 1 is a
representation of one of the pillars just described
as standing in front of Wroxeter church. Both
these pillars are Roman, although their con-
stituent parts did not originally belong to each
other. One of the shafts was fished up out of
the Severn; each, formed of one stone, is six feet
in length. Their bases are similar. The original
of fig. 2 is in the garden of W. H. Oatley, Esq.,
of Wroxeter — a cylindrical stone, with a few
letters engraved on it; this is supposed to have
been a Roman milliarum or mile-stone. Figs. 4
and 5 are also in Mr. Oatley's collection; figs. 3,
6, and 7, preserved by the late Mr. Stanier,
are now in the garden of G. Bather, Esq., of
Wroxeter.

We have said that some of the massive walls
of Uriconium were plastered and painted both
externally and internally. Such was the case
with the wall forming the semi-circular end of
hypocaust K, which had been painted red, with
stripes of yellow. Subjoined are representations
of some fragments of wall-painting found here.

E

Fig. 1 has a light warm ground, the broad central stripe being deep red, on either side of

WALL PAINTING FOUND AT URICONIUM.

which is a thin black stripe. Some of the specimens have a light ground with blue and pink stripes. To judge from other fragments, the walls of some of the rooms appear to have been painted red.

Fig. 2. The ground here is a light warm tint, over which has been washed, rather than painted, a transparent fancy fringe of brown. To guide

the decorator, a circular line has been scratched
in the plaster by some sharp pointed instrument,
a portion of this being represented in the cut as
it appears at the inner edge of the pattern.
In fig. 3 the ground is also light, but this has
apparently a border of raw sienna, upon which
are painted transparent black stripes. Fig. 4 has
an ornament painted in deep red, with paler red
towards the centre, upon a white ground. Fig. 5.
Black stripes, upon an orange and white ground.
Fig. 6. White ground, upon which there is a deep
red pattern; the fragment of stripe to the right is
in raw sienna.

It would be ridiculous to compare such work
with those magnificent specimens of Roman wall
painting uncovered at Pompeii,[1] or even with that
found on the ruined walls of the houses of Roman
London.[2] Yet coarse although those specimens
from Uriconium are, still they are fragments of
mural decoration; nay more, they are painted in
fresco, that is, the colours laid on fine cement
while this was wet, both dried together, and so
became indissolubly united in hard consistency;
an art but lately revived in England, although
practised with success, as it would appear, by our

---

[1] See *Pompeiana, the Topography, Edifices, and Ornaments of
Pompeii*, by Sir WM. GELL; particularly *plates* 39, 40, 41, and
48; the result of excavations since 1819. Lond. 1832.
[2] See example given, p. 59, *Catalogue of the Museum of
London Antiquities*, collected by C. ROACH SMITH. 1854.

Romano-British forefathers in a remote provincial
town on the Welsh border sixteen hundred years
ago. The paint on some of the fragments is in
such good condition that it looks as if it had been
recently laid on.

The reader will have noticed a number of small
holes on the face of the "old wall," *plate* IV.
It is not easy to make out for what purpose these
were left. Many of them go right through the
thickness of the wall. That some of them had
supported the builders' scaffold is evident from
the complete impress of circular poles left in
mortar, but this can hardly have been the case
with all the holes in the old wall, some of which
are regularly built square apertures. The small
shallow hole in the wall above the drain-hole,
represented in p. 40, has evidently been a tenon-
hole to support a cross-beam and its superincumbent weight of wood-work; but not a vestige of
the Roman carpenters' labour remains at Uriconium, it has mouldered into dust.

CHAPTER V.

FICTILE VESSELS.

LET us now proceed to examine various articles that were lately turned up by the spade of the archæologist on that small portion of the site of Uriconium which was recently excavated. Nor let us forget while examining these, that the Roman town was plundered ere it was destroyed ; these relics, therefore, are in all probability merely the refuse of a valuable booty the barbarians carried away. We should bear in mind, also, that very many things doubtless were consumed in the fire that burnt up Uriconium. Nevertheless, some things escaping both the pillage and the fire have come into our hands, and although the great majority of these are grievously mutilated, still a consideration of them is calculated to enlarge our acquaintance with the social life and habits of the Roman conquerors of Britain.

First of all, let us glance at some specimens of the potter's art dug up at Uriconium, and we will begin with the Samian ware. It is a disputed question whether or not Samian ware was made in this country. This particular class of ancient pottery is distinguished from all others by its being covered externally, as well as internally, by a glaze of the colour of red scaling-wax. This peculiar colouring matter was imparted by oxides of lead and iron. The body of the material, of a paler red, is slightly porous, extremely brittle, and sonorous when struck. This ware acquired, it is said, the name "Samian" from having been originally made at Samos. Arctium, the modern Arezzo, in Tuscany, was famous for the manufacture of this particular description of coral-coloured pottery, which is much spoken of by the ancients in their writings, and was very highly prized by them. We may infer the value our Romano-British forefathers set upon the article, from the carefully-mended specimens of Samian ware found at Uriconium : these had been mended by metal rivets. Vessels of Samian ware, endless in the variety both of their shapes and ornamentation, have been found in Britain. Mr. C. Roach Smith states, that on the site of Roman London alone several hundred varieties have been collected, and upwards of three hundred different potters' names. The name of the maker is often stamped in a label across the centre of the inside of the vessel, in a similar manner to this potter's mark, which was found upon one of the pieces of Samian ware

picked up at Uriconium. These ligatured letters probably represent the name TEDDI.

The subject of the embossed groups and figures on many of the Samian vases are taken from the Greek and Roman mythology; others are copies from the masterpieces of ancient art, or illustrate gladiatorial combats, field sports, foliage, etc. Some of the articles in Samian ware dug up at Uriconium, it is painful to relate, represent licentious scenes of an infamous description.

The Samian ware in the museum at Shrewsbury[1] is not first-rate in quality; it had probably been imported into Britain from Gaul. A few examples are given in *plate* IX. The article represented in the upper corner to the left is the remaining side of a vase, about 6¾ inches in diameter; subject, a hunting scene, with bushy tree in centre, the whole being executed in bold relief. In the right-hand corner, in a label just above the rump of the boar, or lion, the potter's name is stamped. By the side of the vase alluded to there is sketched a cracked Samian bowl or vase, 7¼ inches in diameter; this has a floral orna-

---

[1] As the articles were recovered from the site of Uriconium they were removed to the Museum of the Shropshire and North Wales Natural History and Antiquarian Society, on College Hill, Shrewsbury, where they remain. The curator of this museum is Dr. Henry Johnson, to whose kindness, in permitting me to examine and make drawings of the relics from the Roman city, I would here acknowledge my obligations.

mentation in relief. The central fragment is
rather a superior one. A female, with her arms
bound behind her, is represented standing amidst
a variety of animals, all frisking about. Down
in the corner to the right there is a female, apparently hastening to the rescue. The execution is
spirited; it is in high relief.

Of the two lowermost pieces of Samian ware,
the one to the left is a piece of the boldly projecting rim of a well-turned large vase, with
raised leaf ornament. The remaining one is a
plain shallow bowl, about nine inches in diameter.

The annexed represents a fragment closely
resembling Samian ware, found
at Uriconium, which has a rude
incised instead of a projecting
ornament; it may have been of
provincial manufacture, towards
the later period of the Roman occupation of
Britain. There are other specimens of the same
description in the museum at Shrewsbury.

The Samian ware found on Roman sites in this
country, it is most likely, was of foreign make.
There can be little doubt, however, that by far
the larger portion of the so-called Roman vases,
urns, jugs, etc., picked up in Britain, were not
imported, but actually manufactured in this
country before the close of the fifth century. At
Durobricæ, Castor, in Northamptonshire, the late

SAMIAN WARE.

Mr. Artis traced a series of Romano-British potteries upwards of twenty miles along the country bordering on the Nen.[1] There existed in the time of the Romans, also, a vast pottery at Upchurch, on the banks of the river Medway, in Kent; and there were potteries in Lincolnshire, and probably also in Yorkshire, as there certainly were potteries in Salop at that period. From the geological character of the widely separated localities in which the remains of these potteries have been traced, it is evident that the Romans had perseveringly sought out beds of clay peculiarly eligible for the fabrication of fictilo vessels. An inspection of the fragments found at Uriconium will show that there had been in daily use fifteen hundred years ago, even in this provincial town, earthenware good both in quality and design.

The vases manufactured at Castor were of a superior quality; they are usually of a blue-black or slate colour, produced by suffocating the fire of the kiln. Of this particular ware, known as Durobrivæn, the annexed represent a few fragmentary examples, that escaped the destruction of Uriconium.

Fig. 1. This fragment of a cup, or bowl, is of a dark warm grey colour; it has a very peculiar, bold, projecting ornamentation. Fig. 2 is also of

---

[1] For specimens of the interesting remains discovered by Mr. Artis, see *Durobrivæ of Antoninus Identified*. Pl. Lond. 1823.

a dark warm grey colour, subject, dog chasing a
hare, executed in bold relief. The original, from

DUROBRIVÆN WARE.

whence the sketch is made, is about three inches
across. Fig. 3 represents a small blue-black
fragment. Fig. 4 has a dark ground with projecting white slip, which must have been laid on
by hand after the vessel had been fired. In fig. 5
there is also a projecting white slip, but it rests on
a ground of deep red.

The Upchurch ware was not equal to that
manufactured at Castor. It is, however, of a
fine hard texture, is also generally of a blue-
black colour, simple in design, yet extremely
varied in the pattern. A quantity of this ware
was dug up at Wroxeter; subjoined are some
specimens.

Fig. 1 represents the fragment of a good-sized
vase. Fig. 2 represents the nozle and handle of
that which has apparently been an elegantly-

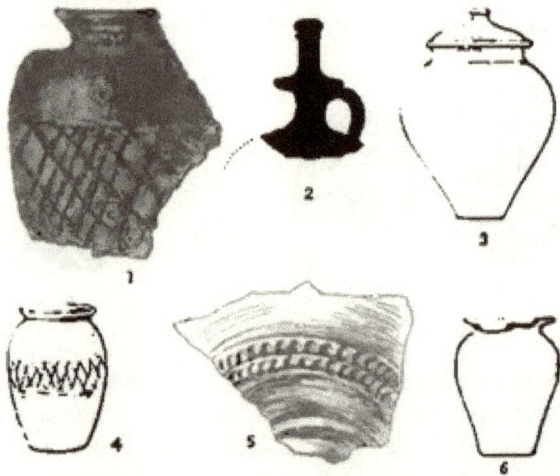

UPCHURCH WARE.

shaped bottle. Figs. 1
and 2 will give the
reader a very good notion of the
dark look of the Upchurch ware;
the other examples are sketched
merely in outline. Figs. 3 and
4 are two small cinerary urns, or
vases. Fig. 5 is a very coarsely
made fragment. Fig. 6 is a mutilated pot or vase, standing about
4½ inches high. Fig. 7 represents
a small flat-bottomed, shallow,

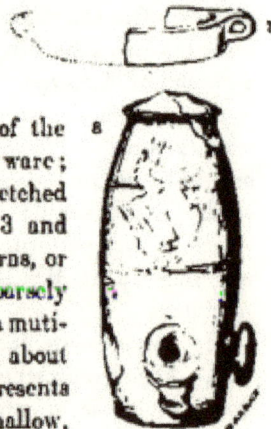

oval-shaped basin, of dark Upchurch ware. Fig. 8. This is a curious article; it is very much mutilated, yet the sketch gives the exact shape. Apparently there has originally been another button-like handle on its left-hand side, and something, probably a spout, with an underneath support, has been broken off in front; behind it is quite plain. It does not appear to have had a hole at the top, nor indeed in any other place, except the one represented. I leave it to the reader to conjecture for what purpose this piece of pottery was formed.

Besides the foregoing classes of earthenware vessels, other descriptions of pottery have been

found on the site of Uriconium. Of the two sketches here given, the one to the left represents a capital double-handled urn, the upper portion of which is a light cream colour, and the lower one

red, over which have been painted a series of
black stripes, now much obliterated. The ornamentation of the upper half of this urn is composed of a series of red spots, carefully picked
out of the white ground by black lines. The
decoration extends even to the handles.[1]

The sketch for the cut on the right was made
from a more rudely formed yet elegant red clay
vase, standing thirteen inches high.[2]

The subjoined is a slightly-made cup, or very
small vase, having three rows of
sharply pointed projections. This
cup stands just 3¼ inches high;
it has a greenish-yellow glaze
spread over both its external
and internal surface.

The recent excavations on the site of Uriconium brought to light large quantities of a
commoner description of pottery, much of which,
doubtless, was made from the clays of the Severn
valley. These more ordinary earthenware vessels
are as various in their shapes as in the purposes for which they had been formed by their

---

[1] This urn was found at Wroxeter previously to the late excavation. It is now in the possession of S. Wood, Esq., of
Shrewsbury, who kindly permitted me to make this drawing
of it.

[2] Also recovered from the site of Uriconium previously to the
late excavations. Now in the possession of W. H. Oatley, Esq.,
of Wroxeter, who obligingly placed his collection from the
Roman city at my disposal.

Romano-British potters. Examples are given in
plate X.

Fig. 1 represents the elegantly-shaped mouth,
neck, and handle of a large pitcher or flagon.
Figs. 2 and 3 were drawn from two nicely-formed
jugs; the former stands ten inches high, and
the latter seven. Fig. 4 represents a small red
earthen bottle; fig. 5 a drinking cup. Fig. 6 is
the twisted handle, in fact all that remains, of a
coarsely-formed large jar; yet there is taste dis-
played in the make even of this very common
article. 7, 7, represent a couple of fragments,
probably, of an amphora for holding wine; the
vessel has been between two and three feet in
height. Figs. 8, 9, represent two small clay
lamps. On the upper side of 8, a small projecting figure, clothed in a tunic, is represented kneel-
ing, and there are three lamp holes. Fig. 9, a
lamp of a different design, has no handle at the
side; there are, however, two small projections at
the top, by which it formerly may have been
suspended. At the bottom of this lamp its maker's
name, MODES, is stamped in projecting letters.
Fig. 10, a side view, and also the bottom, of a
small three-pronged skillet. The sight of fig. 11
transports us in imagination to the kitchens of
Uriconium, for it is the fragment of a colander
for straining vegetables.

The following represent some articles in a white

Plate X.

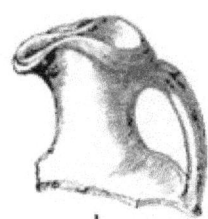

porous ware, made of clay similar to that found
in the neighbourhood of Broseley, Salop. Fig. 1
is the remaining portion of another kitchen uten·

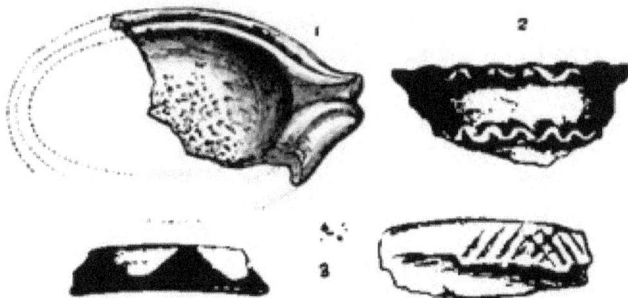

WHITE CLAY WARE.

sil, being a basin-shaped Roman mortaria, supposed to have been used for pounding with a
pestle meat, vegetables, or other articles connected
with cookery. Its interior is studded with small
flint and granite fragments, evidently to promote
a better friction. The number of mortariæ found
in this country would lead one to infer that our
Romano-British forefathers were partial to made
dishes. Fig. 2 is the fragment of a very coarsely
made light clay bowl, ornamented with a double
fringe. Fig. 3 represents all that remains of the
rims of two bowls; the ornamentation of the
fragment to the left is in red; the stripes upon
the other example are of a dirty orange colour.

Now, coarse although these fragments are, still they prove that a painted ware was made in Salop at that early period.

But in vain we search among the relics of Uriconium for fictile vessels equal in beauty to the bowls and vases from Etruria; or for samples of Roman pottery so good even as many found elsewhere in Britain, that are now treasured up in the museums of London and York.

CHAPTER VI.

GLASS.

ALTHOUGH the origin of the manufacture of glass is involved in obscurity, the art, undoubtedly, is of great antiquity. It is one "with which the Egyptians appear to have been acquainted, at least as early as the reign of the first Osirtasen, upwards of 3500 years ago;" in proof whereof, Sir Gardner Wilkinson refers to two paintings at Beni Hassan, representing glass-blowers at work; paintings, which the hieroglyphics that accompany them shew had been executed at the early date mentioned. "We can positively state," continues the authority quoted, "that 200 years after, or about 1500 B.C., they (the Egyptians) made ornaments of glass; a bead bearing a king's name who lived at that period having been found at Thebes."[1]

The superior knowledge which the ancients possessed in glass-making is attested by the cele-

[1] The paintings and the glass bead alluded to are engraved in Sir G. WILKINSON's valuable work on *The Manners and Customs of the Ancient Egyptians*, vol. iii., pp. 89, 90, ed. 1847.

F

brated Portland vase, and that other amphora-
shaped vase exhumed at Pompeii,[1] examples of
themselves sufficient to prove that modern science
has not added much to the perfection attained
2000 years ago in the fabrication of this beautiful
article. The glass-houses of Alexandria, Tyre,
and Sidon enjoyed a high repute among the
ancients. We learn from Pliny that in his time
the manufactories of glass were situated on the
coast in various parts of the Roman empire. He
alludes to the glass manufactories of the Spanish
and Gallic provinces;[2] from whence, doubtless,
numbers of glass vessels were imported into
Britain.

Glass beads or rings in various colours have
frequently been found in tumuli of the early
British period, from which circumstance Pennant
and others have argued that the art of glass-
making was practised in Britain previously to the
Roman conquest. These *glain nadroedh*, Druidic
glass rings, or amulets, most probably, however,
had been obtained by our ancient British forefathers from the Phœnicians, with whom they are

---

[1] Engraved and coloured in Mr. APSLEY PELLATT'S work,
entitled *Curiosities of Glass Making*, London, 1849. The Portland
vase is in the British Museum. It was found about the middle
of the sixteenth century, near Rome, enclosed in a marble sar-
cophagus, within a sepulchral chamber, the tomb, as is supposed,
of Alexander Severus.
[2] PLINY, *Hist. Nat.*, lib. xxxvi., c. 66.

known to have held an intercourse long prior to
the advent of the Romans.[1]
The Romans whilst in Britain manufactured
glass, and a variety of fine specimens have been
found on the sites of the Romano-British houses
and towns. In *plate* XI., subjoined, are represented several articles in glass that were dug up
at Uriconium.

Fig. 1 is a transparent, slightly bluish-green,
thin glass vase; it stands five inches in height,
and is as perfect as when made. This vase was
dug up in the cemetery of Uriconium; when
found it was full of soil, which was everywhere
penetrated by roots of plants. Fig. 2 represents
a pillar moulded Roman glass bowl, 5½ inches in
diameter, also found in the cemetery. According to
a practical authority, pillar moulding is one of the
greatest modern improvements in glass-making;
it was supposed to be a modern invention;[2] such
ancient specimens as this, however, demonstrate
it to be only a revival of a long lost art. Fig. 3,
a transparent, bluish-green, light glass bottle with
narrow neck, height 6½ inches. This was also
found in the cemetery. Fig. 4 represents the
narrow neck (quite four inches long), with remains

---

[1] See BRAND'S *Popular Antiquities*, vol. iii., p. 369, Bohn's ed.,
under heading *Ovum Anguinum*, for the reputed history of the
formation of these rings or beads.
[2] PELLATT'S *Curiosities of Glass Making*, p. 106.

of handle, of that which has apparently been a coarse yet elegantly shaped glass flagon; the colour of this specimen is totally different to any of the others, being purple-brown. Fig. 5 was also dug up in the cemetery; it is a bluish-green glass lachrymatory, so called because such were supposed to contain tears of grief for the departed; the generally received opinion now is, however, that these contained the unguents and aromatics which it was usual to deposit with the dead. Oily matter was detected in one of these small bottles, many of which had evidently been exposed to fire—the fire that had burned the body. Fig. 6 represents a fragment of the side of a thick light blue-green square bottle, having projecting circular ornament; this, therefore, had been blown in a square mould. Fragments of round flat-bottomed bottles were also found at Uriconium. Fig. 7 is a curious piece of colourless ribbed glass. Fig. 8 represents the fragment of a light green glass bowl, studded with rude projecting dots of dark blue or purple glass.

The annexed represents a fine blue glass bead, ornamented with internal zig-zags of white glass.[1] It was picked up out of the midst of the Severn at Wroxeter;

---

[1] This bead is in Mr. Oatley's collection.

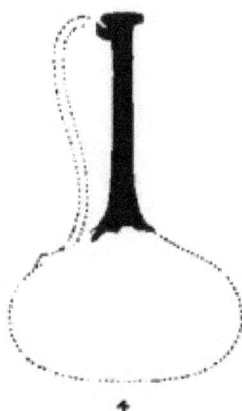

Plate XI.

GLASS.

and in all probability was of Roman make, similar compound-coloured glass beads having been frequently found on the sites of the Roman towns and cemeteries, both in England and on the continent.

It has been previously mentioned, that a quantity of flat window-glass was found during the late excavations, and that to some of the fragments the mortar which had fixed the window into its place still adhered. The article upon glass, in the *Encyclopædia Britannica*, contains the following:—"The Venerable Bede asserts that glass windows were first introduced into England, in the year 674, by the Abbot Benedict, who brought over artificers skilled in the art of making window-glass, to glaze the church and monastery of Wearmouth. Other authorities attribute the introduction of this luxury to Bishop Wilfred, junior, who died in 711. It would thus appear that glass windows were first introduced into England either about the end of the seventh or the beginning of the eighth century. The use of window-glass, however, was then, and for many centuries afterwards, confined entirely to buildings appropriated to religious purposes," etc. Now, with every respect to Venerable Bede's authority, and that of the author of the article in question, the recent excavations made upon the site of Uriconium prove both to be in error; these show

that window-glass was in existence, and made use
of, in this Romano-British town previously to the
end of the fourth century.[1] We would not have
it understood, however, that this window-glass,
or indeed any of the glass found at Uriconium, is
equal to our modern glass in transparent bril-
liancy and that absence from colour which are
the distinguishing traits of recent discoveries; far
from it. Moreover, some of the Roman glass dug
up here has become decomposed, a proof of its
having been defectively made; and the alkali, of
which in part it was composed, through long exposure to the damp earth, has dissolved.

---

[1] Window-glass was found in some of the houses at Pompeii.
Pompeii was destroyed, A.D. 79.

CHAPTER VII.

IRON.

THAT our Romano-British forefathers wrought in iron there is no doubt. The great forest of Anderida, forming the modern Weald of Sussex and Kent, supplied the Romans with iron from a very early period of their occupation of Britain. It was from the ferruginous clays and sands of the Wealden formation, in the vast beds of sandstone constituting what is locally named the Forest Ridge, which reaches at Crowborough an elevation of 804 feet above the level of the ocean; from those beds, extending inland from Hastings towards the west, known among geologists as the Hastings Sand, it was that the Roman miners extracted their iron.[1] Large beds of iron scoriæ, technically termed slag, amid which Roman coins and fragments of pottery mingle, have also been found in Northumberland and the north of England.

---

[1] For an account of the extinct furnaces and forges of the Weald, the reader is referred to page 85, *et supra*, of *Contributions to Literature*, by M. ANTONY LOWER, M.A., F.S.A., where will be found reprinted that paper on the Southern Ironworks, which originally appeared in vol. ii. of the *Collections* of the Sussex Archæological Society.

But it is to Gloucestershire and the west of England that wo must look chiefly for evidences of the Roman iron-works. Very numerous remains of Roman mines, or scowles, as they are popularly termed in these parts, exist on the high ground in the neighbourhood of the Forest of Dean, and along the banks of the romantic river Wye. There are immense deposits of iron scoriæ, or cinders, from the Roman works scattered over the country to the north of the Wye, between Monmouth and Bridstow: aged, gnarled oaks grow over these remains.

In the early days of the iron trade, ere the huge "blast furnace," with its improvements of coke and steam-power had been thought of, to produce iron our forefathers erected rude, low, conical furnaces upon elevated sites near forests, in order to obtain a more perfect blast and the necessary charcoal. An examination of the cinders from these primitive works has led to the conclusion that the Romans smelted their ore imperfectly. So much iron, indeed, is left in the old scoriæ, that it has often been found profitable to re-smelt them; and it is computed that in Dean Forest alone twenty furnaces, for a period of upwards of 300 years, were supplied with Roman and Danish cinders, as a substitute for iron-ore.

Worcester and its neighbourhood, in the Roman

era, was a district of iron-works and forges, sub-
ordinate to the great district of the Forest of
Dean. Doubtless some of the iron implements
found at Uriconium had been fabricated by the
famed Roman smiths of *Alauna*, Alcester.

On *plate* XII. are represented a number of iron
implements and weapons, which having been dug
up on the site of Uriconium, were deposited in
the museum at Shrewsbury, where they remain,
yet in a corroded state.

The implements drawn on the upper half of
plate XII. apparently were formed for useful or
domestic use; the huge chopper in the right-hand
corner might, however, have been applied to a
more deadly purpose. Fig. 1 is the blade of a
knife, of which the handle has perished; the bone
handle still remains on fig. 2. Fig. 3 is a small
knife, like those used by our cobblers for cutting
leather; it has a screw wherewith to twist into
the bone or wooden handle. Fig. 4 is very like
a modern brad-awl; the bone handle of this
article is still intact. Fig. 5 is a trowel, exactly
like those which our modern bricklayers make
use of.

Of the two steel axe-heads represented, the one
to the right is a heavy flat-headed article, not
much unlike the axe-heads sometimes found in
Saxon graves; but the cutting end of the Teutonic weapon, curved out into sharper points, is

decidedly the more formidable weapon.[1] To the right of the axe-head is a prick-spur, beneath which again is represented the bit of a Roman bridle.

The lowermost row of articles represented in *plate* XII. unquestionably were offensive weapons all of them; fig. 6 evidently being a dangerous one. This is flat-headed, and about ten inches long; the nail that had helped to constitute the lowermost ring which formerly held its long wooden shaft still remains. The spear-head drawn next is more than ten inches in length. Those are two arrow-heads that are drawn in the lower-most right-hand corner.

One would suppose, from the Romans having been such a martial race, that they would have left behind them quantities of the armour which they wore, and weapons both offensive and defensive with which they had fought. Yet curious to relate, such is not the case; there has come down to us but a very meagre list of articles connected with the warfare of our Roman conquerors, unless indeed, as some learned antiquarians contend, those fine bronze shields, swords, and spear-heads, that have hitherto ranked as of British make, are incorrectly described as such, and in reality are

---

[1] The heads of two Saxon axes, one taken from a Saxon bar-row in the Isle of Thanet, and the other found in a grave at Selzen in Rhenish Hesse, are represented in chap. xiv. of *The Celt, the Roman, and the Saxon*, by THOMAS WRIGHT, M.A., F.S.A., etc.

Plate XII.

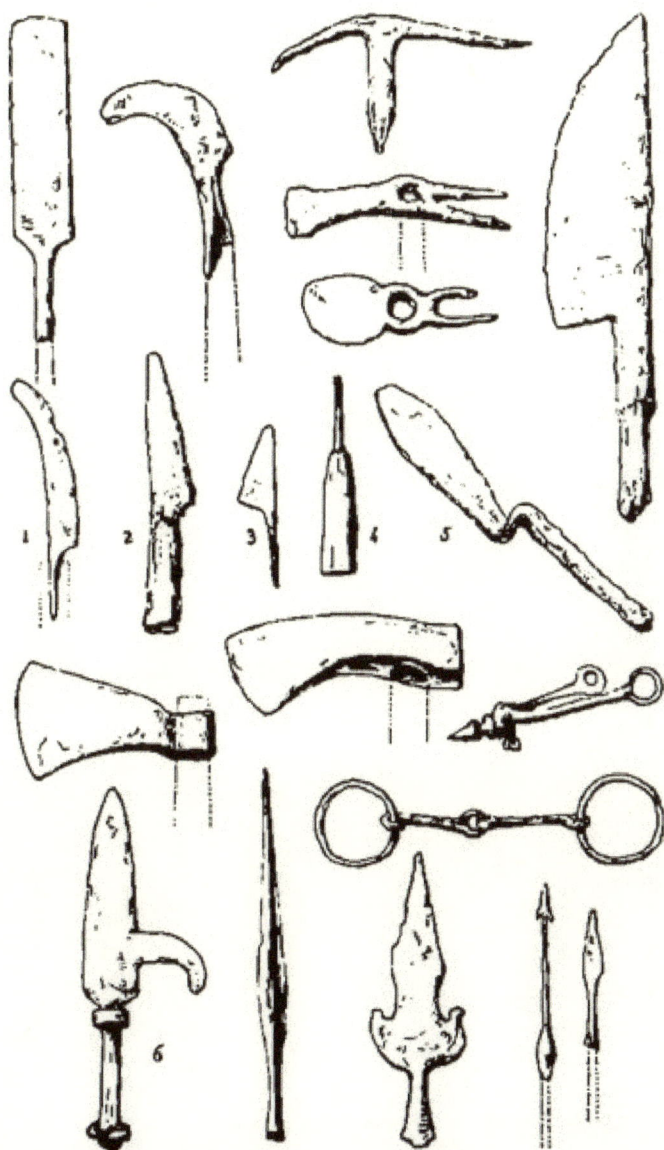

IRON IMPLEMENTS AND WEAPONS.

weapons of Roman manufacture. It is a significant circumstance, however, that as yet no bronze weapon of war has been dug up at Uriconium. But there was found the iron tire of a wheel three feet three inches in diameter and 1½ inch in breadth, with two iron hoops, supposed to have belonged to the nave of the same chariot wheel. The space between the hoops had apparently been filled up with solid wood-work, for, between two hoops of another nave, fragments of wood still remain.

Besides those represented in *plate* XII. there were some other iron articles picked up during the late excavations that deserve to be mentioned; such as that small iron trident and fragment of chain alluded to in p. 28; iron bolts; T-shaped iron stanchions; and there was the *umbilicus*, or hinge, for a door. The subjoined represent three Roman keys: the first, apparently, is a large door-key; a small one of the same design was also found. At the handle end of the central key there is a circular hole, wherewith to suspend it, with the bunch, to the girdle: some keys of this description found had three prongs; this one

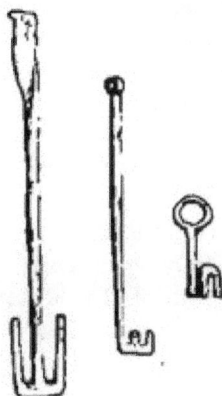

has only two. The key to the right is a small finger key. Numbers of keys are found on the Roman sites; they present the greatest diversity in their patterns, many of them being intricate. During the late excavations there was found a corroded mass of iron, supposed to be the remains of a Roman padlock.

A number of iron nails were dug up at Uriconium, of which some, similar in shape to the great headed one here represented, were of an immense size. The nail in the centre presents the usual shape however; it is round-headed with a square shank. Some of this kind were six inches in length. One of these long nails was taken to a smith, who hammered it out into a steel point, and pronounced it made of excellent iron. In the museum there are some little flat-headed nails also, of the size and shape of our tin-tacks; one of this latter description of Roman nail is represented; the original, however, is not made of iron but bronze.

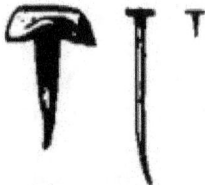

Only one hammer was found on the site of the old Roman town; it was of lead, and of the shape here figured.

CHAPTER VIII.

DRESS—PERSONAL ORNAMENT—THE TOILETTE.

STRICTLY speaking, not a single article of clothing has escaped the ravages by fire and time to which the Roman city has been subjected; like the wooden moveable furniture of the Romano-British houses, the dresses of their occupants have perished. We partly glean, however, from the impression of the nails on this fragment of a Roman tile dug up here, the shape of the sole of a Roman shoe or sandal.

As the clothing of the Romans consisted for the most part of garments that hung or wrapped loosely about their bodies, they would require various devices to fasten and hold them together, and this will account for the number of fibulæ or brooches that are found upon all Roman sites. Of those found at Uriconium, which are very ordinary examples, the annexed represent a few specimens.

Fig. I is a massive bronze fibula 3½ inches long,
having part of the pin that had fastened it

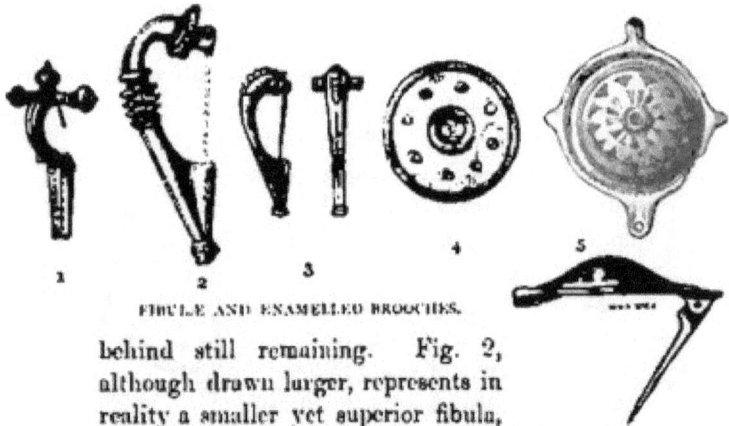

FIBULÆ AND ENAMELLED BROOCHES.

behind still remaining. Fig. 2,
although drawn larger, represents in
reality a smaller yet superior fibula,
also manufactured in bronze. Fig. 3 is a small
bronze fibula, the pin of which still remains perfect. Fig. 4, drawn the size of the original,
represents a circular bronze brooch with studs,
within the intermediate space between which
remain portions of an enamelled paste that
glistens like mother of pearl. Fig. 5, another
circular bronze brooch, drawn also as large as the
original; on the front there is a design executed
in enamel, scarlet and blue alternately, in an
inner circle, surrounded by another circle of blue
triangular ornaments. The pin still works perfectly on its hinge.

The annexed represents a Roman circular bronze fastener with a bent pin, as sharp as when new.

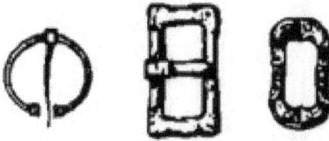

To the right of it are drawn two bronze buckles found at Wroxeter in 1860.

Nor had the utility of the button as a means of fastening been overlooked by the Romans, for here is the fragment of a jet one dug up at Uriconium. Adjoining it is represented a very neatly formed bronze stud or button.

A number of bone and bronze pins, which had been used by the Romano-British females who resided at Uriconium, to fasten the knot of hair behind the head, and for other purposes, were found. Roman pins are often elaborately ornamented; only very inferior ones were picked up during the late excavations. The pins drawn on the next page are all made of bone; the one on the left-hand side is stained black. There were a number of slender bronze pins also found.

Respecting those articles which appropriately may be classed under the head of personal ornaments, it may be mentioned that several bracelets (*armillæ*) were found of different patterns, some

ROMAN BONE PINS DUG UP ON THE SITE OF URICONIUM.

plain, others twisted. The annexed cut represents a bronze bracelet, of which several specimens were found. Beneath is drawn a fragment of twisted bronze that seems, from its comparative thickness, to have belonged to a *torques* or collar. Roman torques and armillæ occur in gold, silver, and bronze; those found at Wroxeter are very inferior.

Various kinds of finger rings were dug up, some being made of jet. In the Roman time buttons, beads, rings, and such like articles of personal ornament were manufactured apparently on an extensive scale in *gagates*, jet, Kennel or Kimmeridge coal. The ancients, as we learn from Pliny, set an additional value on articles made of this material, from the notion that it possessed the virtue of driving away serpents, a belief which obtained currency also in the time of Venerable Bede, who, describing the various mineral products of Britain, says, "It has much and excellent jet, which is black and sparkling, glittering at the fire, and when heated drives away serpents."[1] In the secluded valleys that open out into the Kimmeridge and Worthbarrow bays, on the Isle of Purbeck, Dorsetshire, there are found, a little below the surface, extensive beds of small pieces of Kimmeridge coal, bearing indisputable marks of having been turned on the lathe. From the circumstance that fragments of Roman pottery mingle with this refuse, it has been conjectured that here we have traces of one of the Romano-British jet manufactories.

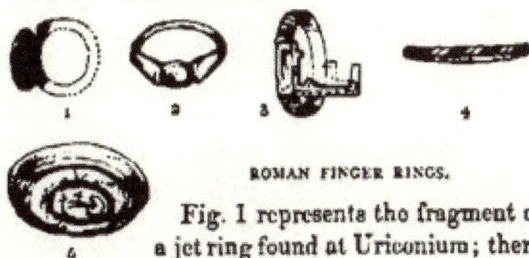

ROMAN FINGER RINGS.

Fig. 1 represents the fragment of a jet ring found at Uriconium; there

---

[1] BEDE, *Eccl. Hist.*, B. i, c. i.

was another capital example. Fig. 2, a plain silver ring. Fig. 3 is a bronze ring that has formerly had an ornamental projection, the greater portion of which is now lost. Fig. 4, a ring composed of twisted bronze and iron wire. Fig. 5, an iron signet ring, an uncommon article; the device is a hart escaping from a snail's shell.

Besides the one just alluded to, other intaglios, or engraved stones, have been picked up on the site of Uriconium at former periods. The annexed represents an intaglio found in 1840. It is engraved upon a black stone, having a vein of white on its face; the cutting shows up a black figure. Underneath it is another ordinary intaglio, curved on a bright red stone. Drawings of other Roman engraved stones, found at Uriconium, can be seen in *plate* X., Vol. XIX., of *Journal of the British Archæological Association*, but the originals having been carried away, they appear to have almost lost connection with the locality whence they were derived.[1]

Pliny, who lived A.D. 23-79, speaks of the love of precious stones as being in his time a "uni-

---

[1] The original of the engraved stone in the ring is in the Shrewsbury Museum; the other two intaglios represented I saw at the residence of W. H. Oatley, Esq., at Wroxeter.

versal passion." Describing some of the engraved
stones possessed by celebrated men, he mentions
that the Emperor Augustus used a stone with the
figure of a sphinx engraved on it, as his signet;
but as this gave rise to jokes on the enigmatical
language in which he used to write, Augustus
abandoned the sphinx, and adopted as his signet
a stone with the head of Alexander the Great
engraved on it. Their love for the glyptic art
the Romans carried with them into the remotest
corners of their empire; hence it comes to pass
that Roman intaglios are often turned up by the
plough and spade in Britain. "When we con-
sider the variety of such monuments found in
Britain, and the numbers — not forgetting that
the mere fact of so many being found amounts to
a proof that they were in very common use — it
leads us naturally to raise the question, Was the
glyptic art itself established in this distant province?" a question which Mr. Wright answers
in the affirmative, giving as his reason for so
doing, that "there is a certain character stamped
on most of the engraved stones we find here
which seems to mark it as provincial art."[1] The
belief in the supernatural agency of engraved
stones, or gems, prevailed universally throughout

[1] *Essay on Roman Engraved Stones found on the Site of Uriconium, at Wroxeter, Salop, by* T. WRIGHT, Esq., M.A., F.S.A.
See *Journal of the British Arch. Assoc*, vol. xix., pp. 106—111.

tho middlo ages; a circumstance to which we owo the preservation of many a gem of ancient art.

Thero was dug up on the site of Uriconium, during the late excavations, a bronze heart-shaped pendant, of which tho subjoined cuts represent three sides. It is partially ena-melled in front, tho upper central portion consisting of blue, whilst tho half obliterated circle at the lower extremity shows scarlet enamel. A series of small circles are engraved on the bronze portion of the front, which ovidently opened and shut, as a square aperture remains at the side, where tho spring probably had formerly pro-jected. The back is plain, but perforated by two holes; there has in all likelihood been a third hole lower down, the space it occupied being now covered by an adhesion that also obscures the lower parts in front. This article is hollow, doubtless for the purpose of en-closing perfumes or amulets.[1]

The excavators also picked up this curious skiff-

---

[1] A bronze enamelled pendant similar to this, found at Reculver, in Kent, is engraved and explained in Mr. C. Roach Smith's Essay on that Roman station.

shaped bronze article, which, from its size and peculiar make, seems adapted to suspend from a lady's arm. It has a lid, fastened down by a small flat bolt, seen through the aperture in the lower sketch; the end of the bolt is at A. When found it contained coins. Can this be a lady's purse?[1]

The three small ornaments here represented may have been personal ones. The first is composed of two separate bits of lead, the lowermost hanging by a hook from the upper one; the second represents a sharply moulded bronze ornament; the third, composed of the same metallic fusion, has a circular hole at the top, whereby it has formerly been suspended.

Glass beads, of various colours and sizes, were dug up. Some of these, made to string together, doubtless had once hung around the necks or arms of Romano-British ladies; nevertheless, the beads are inferior ones.

As connected with the toilette, the articles here

---

[1] A very perfect bronze vessel, of exactly the same form as the one engraved on p. 84, and containing Roman gold and silver coins, was discovered in the crevice of a rock at Thorngrafton, near Hexham, in Northumberland, in the year 1837.

represented may next be considered. These are a couple of combs, made of bone, found on the site of the Roman city. The comb drawn in the uppermost sketch is an elaborate affair, consisting of a central piece or pieces, with teeth; the upper portion being strengthened in front and behind by transverse pieces of ornamented bone, rivetted together by now much corroded iron rivets; three of the rivets are represented. The smaller comb is neatly formed. These sketches are rather less than two-thirds the size of the originals.

This circular sketch represents a Roman *speculum*, or mirror, of which more than one example was found at Wroxeter. It consists of a thin polished plate of white metal—tin, with a slight mix-

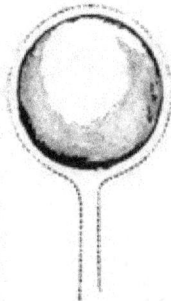

ture of copper. Doubtless, the article formerly was surrounded with a wooden frame, to which had been attached a handle. Although this mirror has been buried under ground so many ages, it still reflects distinctly.

The cut annexed represents a pair of small Roman bronze tweezers, for eradicating superfluous hairs. This is not above two inches in length.

Of the following sketches, fig. 1 represents an article found at Uriconium, and now in the Shrewsbury Museum. It is a flat, slightly curved piece of iron, 4½ inches long. On one side teeth-like indentations are visible; at either end is a projection, with holes, through which rivets or nails have been driven, to fasten it probably to some wooden handle that has long since perished. The circular hole on the left-hand side, through which the nail went, is broken; the nail-head still remains in the hole to the right. Some have concluded that the article alluded to is the remains of a saw; yet, although not of the usual shape, it more likely is the remains of a strigil.

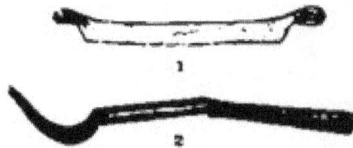

Fig. 2 represents an undoubted bronze Roman strigil; this latter, with some other relics from

the Roman town, is preserved in the library of
the Shrewsbury Grammar School.[1] The strigil
was used for scraping the skin of the bather after
he had been put into a state of perspiration in
the hot bath; it was made use of also by the
Greeks and Romans, to scrape off the moisture
which exuded from the skin during gymnastic
exercises. Generally made of iron or bronze, the
instrument had a curved hollow blade; much
more gently curved than the one represented,
which has violently been bent, and broken off at
the point. The handle of the strigil was often
covered with slight protuberances, to prevent its
slipping in the hand, and so scratching the person
to whose skin it was applied; the handle of the
strigil which we have represented is, however,
quite plain.[2]

Among the numerous articles dug up by the
excavators is a curious decomposed mass, supposed to be the remains of a box of ointment;
yet whether this really contains the remains of
Roman hair-pomade or not, I cannot undertake
to determine.

---

[1] To the courtesy of the Rev. H. Whitehead Moss, Head
Master of the Shrewsbury Grammar School, the author is in-
debted for permission to examine and make drawings from these
relics.

[2] A very perfect Roman strigil, discovered at Reculver, is
represented in plate VII. of Mr. C. Roach Smith's work on that
castrum.

CHAPTER IX.

MISCELLANEOUS.

THERE has been dug up on the site of the provincial town of Uriconium a miscellaneous collection of articles, which, attentively considered, whether in relation to their scientific or artistic design, the diverse materials in which they are fabricated, or the varied purposes and ideas their use in the aggregate involves, cannot fail to show how extensive must have been the trade and manufacture, and how comparatively great the civilisation which prevailed in Britain during that period when it continued a Roman province.

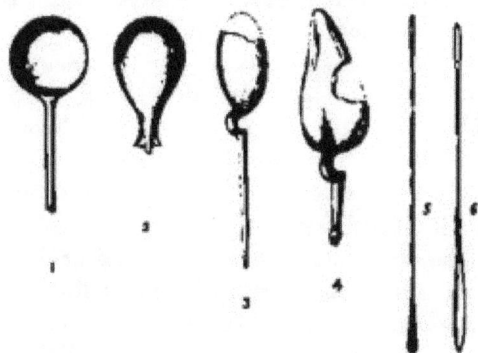

The foregoing represent various kinds of Roman *ligulæ*, or spoons. Fig. 1 is apparently the fragment of a circular-bowled *cochlear*, the handle of which, terminating in a point, was used for picking snails or periwinkles out of their shells. Artificially-fed snails are said to have been considered a dainty by the Romans ; a large species of snail is still found existing about some Roman stations. Fig. 2 represents the back of a differently shaped spoon, the handle of which is broken off. Fig. 3, an egg-shaped spoon, having an abrupt curve in its handle close to the bowl, wherewith seemingly to suspend the spoon from the rim of the cup ; the leaf-shaped example, marked 4, has a similar curve. Figs. 5 and 6 are diminutive spoons, for scooping out of long-necked bottles. The foregoing are in bronze ; iron spoons, however, were also found, among which is a large ladle. There is another mutilated ladle, in block tin.

The annexed represents the fragment of a beautifully formed cup, or small bowl, that almost appears silver-plated, so bright it is on the exterior. Formed of white bronze, this is a brittle article.

The explorers discovered a remarkably well-made copper cup, and one made of lead. Some large plates of lead were also found, yet to what purpose these had originally been applied is un-

91

certain. The existence of lead mines in the
neighbouring Stipperstones, where Roman pigs of
lead have been found, may account for so much
lead being dug up during the late excavations.

That our modern steelyard is merely a copy of
one used in Britain 1500 years ago, the subjoined sketch of a steelyard, found amid the

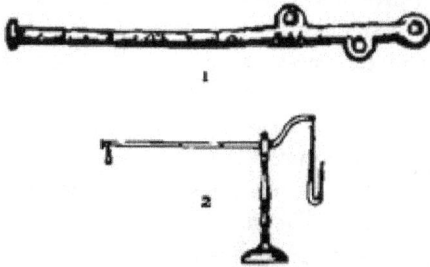

1

2

ruins of this Roman city, will prove. Fig. 2
is a patent letter-weighing machine, drawn in
order that the reader may compare it with the
Roman steelyard. The steelyard found at Uriconium is notched and half-notched, and it has
likewise fractional division marks on it.

Several weights were picked up. One, in
lead, weighs 20¼ ozs.; another leaden weight

was marked II, it weighed 2½ ozs.: stone weights

wore also found. Four differently shaped weights are here represented : three are stone ones ; the lowermost is the leaden weight, marked II. No scales have hitherto been turned up on this site, yet that the use of the scale (*libra*, the balance) was known to the Romans is certain, from allusions to it in their writings, and the frequency with which scales are represented on coins and other works of art.

One of the most curious articles found is the one here drawn, which is generally believed to be a bronze Roman lancet. When discovered, this was embedded in remains evidently of the case it had fitted into. The flat blade at the lower extremity is pointed like a lancet, and is very sharp.

Several iron and bronze styli have been picked up on the site of Uriconium. When an educated Roman wished to communicate with his friend by writing, he took a book-like tablet, consisting of some thin wooden leaves fastened together, over the surface of which wax was spread. With an instrument called a stylus, one end of which was sharply pointed and the other end flat, the Roman then wrote or scratched what he had to say upon the wax, when tying the tablet together by a string or thread, he sealed the knot, and sent his servant with the internally

inscribed tablet to the proper party. Having
perused the letter, the friend, if he wished to
return an answer, could do so by erasing with
the flat end of the stylus the previously written
lines on the wax, and substituting any others he
might choose. The accompanying illustra-
tion of a bronze stylus found here, the
reader will notice, has one extremity sharp-
pointed, whilst the other is flattened. We
talk of a man's style of writing; here undoubtedly we have the derivation of the
term. Again, we speak of stabbing with the
pen, a metaphorical expression of course;
yet in the days when sharp-pointed bronze and
iron styli were in vogue, a vicious writer might,
and in fact occasionally did, give his antagonist
the *quietus* with an instrument such as is represented above.

Sewing appears to have been a common occupation of the Roman ladies
in Britain. Here are a couple of bone
needles that were dug up at Uriconium. The broken one to the right is
a double-eyed needle, the remaining
portion being 4½ inches in length.
Scissors have been found on Roman
sites; as yet, however, none have been
picked up here.

The annexed represents a large horn

skewer, having a hole drilled in the centre of its
round head.

Several bronze statuettes were found, two
of which, a small Venus and a Mercury, are
preserved in the Museum at Shrewsbury.
The Venus is a badly executed copy of one
of the masterpieces of Greek art, the atti-
tude being the same as that of the Venus de
Medici. The bronze Mercury alluded to is
here represented, fig. 1; it stands 3¼ inches
high. A small mutilated figure of Diana, in
Mr. Oatley's collection, from which fig. 2 was
drawn, is the best executed work of art that has
hitherto been dug up on the site of the Roman

1   2

town. The latter statuette, also in bronze, is
about 3 inches in height.

Among the curiosities picked up by the excava-

tors was a small head rudely carved in sandstone;
it may have formed part of the architectural
ornamentation of some building.

The quern appears to have been an article
connected with the ordinary domestic life of the
Romans in Britain, stone querns, or hand-mills,
having been found on the Roman sites. The
lower stone was stationary, the upper one revolved
in a socket formed by the other. Several Roman
querns were dug up here. Subjoined is a specimen. A dark granulated stone; this is pointed as
here drawn, pointed in fact ac-
cording to the same scientific
principle a miller adheres to
when he points his mill-stone
now-a-days.

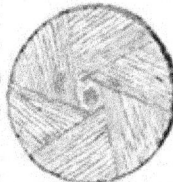

A number of roundels, or but-
tons, were found that had been turned on the
lathe; some in bone, others in earthenware.
Many of the roundels had a hole in the centre;
these had probably been used in some game. The
annexed cut represents a beautifully turned bone
roundel, with hole in centre.
This example is 1½ inch in diameter, others are of a lesser size.
Some of these bone buttons, or
roundels, are plain and flat, others
are convex, and ornamented with
four or more circles. The earthenware roundels
are larger.

Part of a remarkably well-turned bone hilt of
a Roman sword was found.

The accompanying repre-
sent a large, but rather
rudely formed, red earthen
bead. It is 1¾ inch in diameter, and has a hole
pierced right through its centre.[1]

We have already noticed a tile over which an
ox-foot must have trod ere the tile was burnt;
other tiles that were dug up had the impression
of foot of the sheep, dog, pig, and horse.

A vast collection of bones of various animals
were exhumed. Among these were legs of the
fighting cock, with very large natural spurs;
skulls of dogs, one being that of the mastiff kind
of an unknown species. There were also the
bones of the horse, the ox, roe, red-deer, numerous remains of the wild boar, and crania of the
Bos longifrons, a species of ox that is now extinct.
The forehead of several of these crania bear
evidence of the blow that took the life; the flat
square end of that heavy-looking axe-head de-
picted in *plate* XII., fitting singularly well into
one of the huge fractures. Fragments of the
horn of a species allied to the elk of Ireland
(*strongylocerus spelæus*) were found; besides nu-

---

[1] In the possession of S. Wood, Esq., of Shrewsbury.

merous remains of small animals and birds,
quantities of oyster shells were dug up.

Amid the miscellaneous collection of objects
exhumed at Uriconium is a square slab of smooth
whitish stone, one side of which
is flat, the edges of the other
being bevelled off as here represented. This slab is 2¾ inches
long by 2½ broad, and about half
an inch thick. The fragment of
another similar slab was also found; this latter,
however, was much worn away towards the middle by friction. An examination of the worn
slab led to the discovery of remains of colour on
it, from which it is inferred that those were
painters' palettes. Curiously enough, on the
back of the slab sketched, there is a minute inscription in a label, which, according to Mr. Roach
Smith, reads ꟇICLNIVMA, a contraction for
Decinici manu. "Dicinivus," says an eminent
antiquarian, "was probably an artist of Uriconium, to whom this palette belonged, and who
wished to establish his claim to it by writing his
name on the back, in doing which he adopted the
formula in which the potters' names were stamped
on the Samian ware."[1]

[1] See Papers on "Uriconium," 2nd art., the Inscriptions, by
THOMAS WRIGHT, Esq., F.S.A., in vol. xv., *Journal of the
British Archæological Association.*

Several whetstones were found, and they dug
up the stone handle of a knife, and a touchstone.
In his guide to the ruins of Uriconium, Mr.
Wright draws attention, in the catalogue of
Wroxeter antiquities in the museum at Shrewsbury, to "a cock made of lead, a child's toy."
The many, we fear, will fail to perceive a resem-
blance to chanticleer in said piece of lead; certain,
however, it is that such toy-like articles have been
found on Roman sites.[1]
Respecting the oculist's stamp engraved in
p. 15, this was doubtless used to impress the name
of the medicine, and that of its maker, on the pot
or packet containing the preparation. At least
sixty Roman oculists' stamps have been picked
up in Italy, Germany, France, and England.
These, in general, are of a square or oblong
shape, the peculiarity of the one found at Uriconium consists in its circular form. From the
number of oculists' stamps discovered, it has been
inferred that diseases of the eyes were prevalent
throughout the western provinces of the Roman
Empire; yet, whether such was the case or not,
to judge from the phraseology of the round stamp
alluded to, it would seem that a quack doctor

---

[1] There is a Roman child's toy, formed like a cock, in the
British Museum; another veritable cock-toy, which was picked
up along with other leaden toys for children among the ruins
of the Roman city of Magna at Kenchester, is represented in
p. 126 of vol. xxxvii., *Gentleman's Magazine*, New Series.

resided at Uriconium, and from thence, as a
centre, dispersed abroad his pretended efficacious
wares.

A specimen of hepatic iron ore and one of
barytes, or heavy spar, brought from the site
of Uriconium, can be seen in the museum at
Shrewsbury.

CHAPTER X.

COINS.

THE authentic information which coins supply
is of the utmost value in illustrating history;
moreover, numismatic monuments being in their
nature imperishable, are very useful whereby
to correct that tendency to fable and romance
which too often appears in dissertations relating
to ancient times. As Englishmen, we are spe-
cially interested in such coins as refer to the
early history of our ancestors.

At one time it was assumed that there was no
stamped currency in this country prior to the
invasion of Britain by the Romans; yet numismatic researches seem to have established the fact
that coins, rude imitations apparently of Greek
ones, were minted in Britain before Caesar landed:
this, however, is a disputed question. That there
was a British coinage in circulation prior to the
military occupation of this country by the
Romans,[1] however, admits of no doubt; the coins

[1] That is prior to A.D. 43, in the autumn of which year Aulus
Plautius, landing with his army in Britain, overran its south-
eastern portion.

of the British princes Tasciovanus and Cunobeline
are numerous, those of the latter being well
executed. Yet these appear to have been the
last of the British series, which soon afterwards
was superseded by the Roman money.

According to the Rev. Beale Poste, the name
Uriconium is expressed by the word "VRICON,"
"RICON," etc., upon four various types of "ancient British" coins. The coins referred to are
all in gold; the inscriptions on them are in the
Celtic language, in a dialect much resembling
the modern Welsh or Irish. Mr. Poste contends
that the word TASCIO, which is read on these
coins, implies the same as the Latin word Im-
perator, in the sense not of emperor, but as ruler
or commander merely. "It may be observed,"
adds this numismatist, "that the workmanship of
all the specimens is somewhat roughly executed,
though certainly the figures are sketched out
with considerable spirit. The obverses, or front
faces of the coins, display a horseman, with shield
and helmet, galloping rapidly to the left, holding
some implement in his right hand, probably a
carnyx or Celtic war-trumpet, with which the
leaders of the ancient Britons were often pro-
vided. He is looking back, and appears to be
waving to his men to follow on. The reverse
delineates a row of five spears, placed upright
against apparently some framework; and from

one side of these projects another representation
of the Celtic carnyx, or war-trumpet. In all
these specimens there is delineated a double
tablet, terminated at each end in two peaks, and
placed in front of the rows of spears. On this
double tablet the inscription is inserted in two lines,
one word in each," thus ᵀᴬˢᶜᴵᴼⱽ_ᴿᴵᶜᴼᴺ, with variations.
These coins are assigned by Mr. Poste to Cunobeline, and he expresses it as his opinion, that
the chances of war may have thrown Uriconium
within the power of that British prince.[1]

Able numismatists, combating Mr. Poste's
theory, have given a very different interpretation
of the legend TASCIO VRICON, rendering the
former name into that of the British prince Tasciovanus, father of Cunobeline; and contending
that VRICON represents the name of some
British town, certainly not Uriconium.[2]

Like some other legends which are as yet but
imperfectly understood, the ones in question
afford a wide field for speculative theory. It

[1] Mr. Beale Poste's paper, with an engraving of one of the British gold coins referred to, will be found in the *Journal of the British Archaeological Association*, vol. xviii., p. 75, *et seq*.
[2] Mr. Poste's views respecting the Celtic coinage are the subject of numerous learned controversial papers, scattered throughout the *Numismatic Chronicle*, and other kindred publications. See article "On some Coins of Tasciovanus, with the legend VER BOD," read before the Numismatic Society, March 25, 1858, by JOHN EVANS, F.S.A. *Numismatic Chron.* vol. xx.

would follow, from Mr. Poste's argument, that
Uriconium originally was a town not of Roman
but British founding. It is certain, however,
that no relics of an early British character were
discovered during the recent explorations; and,
notwithstanding the large number of Roman
coins that have been found here, only one single
early British or Gaulish coin, presently to be
alluded to, has been picked up on the site of
Uriconium. So far, therefore, Mr. Poste's in-
genious argument rests upon a very slender basis
of fact.

I am not aware of any of that peculiar species
of money known as *Ring Money*, common to the
Teutonic as to the Celtic tribes, having ever been
found at Wroxeter.

"Among a quantity of coins," says Mr. Wright,
"found on the site of Uriconium, in the possession of Mr. W. H. Oatley, of Wroxeter, are a
silver British (or Celtic, for it was perhaps
Gaulish) coin, and a Roman consular coin, also
of silver. The British coin is of the same type
as some gold coins found in Kent, and represented
in Mr. Roach Smith's *Collectanea Antiqua*, vol. i.
pl. vii. figs. 1 to 6. The other coin is one of the
most common consular denarii, and was no doubt
in circulation during a long period. These Celtic
coins, which appear to have belonged to the
earliest period of the Roman domination, were

also, no doubt, in circulation long afterwards; and the discovery of them in any particular spot is no proof that they were deposited there at the time when they were fresh struck. In this case the coin accords with the information we gain from Ptolemy, that Viroconium was one of the oldest of the Roman towns in Britain."[1]

The mintage of the Roman conquerors was very superior to that Gaulish and British coinage which it superseded. The first Roman coin having allusion to Britain bears the name of the Emperor Claudius; and on its reverse the inscription DE BRITANN, on the front of a triumphal arch, surmounted by an equestrian statue between two trophies—a deeply interesting coin, since, without doubt, it commemorates the triumph decreed by the Roman senate to Claudius, and celebrated in the year A.D. 44, on account of his victory over our ancient British forefathers.

Roman coins, both consular and imperial, but especially the latter, are found throughout England in vast numbers. They occur in gold, silver, and brass, the gold and silver being about the size of our sixpence, but much thicker; the brass accord in size with our penny, halfpenny, and farthing, and being classified in three series, are called first, second, and third, or large, middle,

[1] Extract from article on Uriconium, in *Journal of the British Archæological Association*, vol. xv., p. 208, *note*.

and small. Coins of intermediate dimensions,
however, also occur; those of the later times of
the Roman Empire being—the gold coins, less in
weight yet apparently larger; silver ones, thinner
and executed in lower relief; while the Roman
brass coins decrease to a minute size. There are
likewise numerous examples of ancient spurious
Roman money, in lead, iron, and brass, plated
with silver. In page 13, allusion is made to a
quantity of clay moulds for forging Roman coins
that were found at Wroxeter.

From time immemorial numbers of Roman
coins have been found on the site of Uriconium.
Among these is the full-faced coin of Carausius,
now in the British Museum.

Carausius, celebrated as a skilful pilot and
valiant soldier, was appointed admiral of the
Roman fleet stationed off Boulogne, to check the
ravages of the German pirates; a trust, however,
which he clandestinely employed to gain for
himself vast riches. It having been reported to
the emperors that their admiral was unworthy of
the confidence reposed in him, they attempted to
apprehend their servant; but Carausius, receiving
intelligence of his danger, by a bold effort eluded
their endeavour. He sailed over to Britain with
the Roman fleet, and called upon the Britons,
oppressed by the Roman governor and his subor-
dinates, to aid him in throwing off the yoke of

the tyrant. Claiming for himself the title of
Augustus, here, in his island home, the "arch-
pirate," as he was styled, defied the vengeance
of the emperors. It was in the year 287 that
Carausius steered for Britain. The bold usurper
firmly grasped the sceptre of this nascent British
Empire for seven years. He drove back the
Caledonians in the north; in the south he courted
an alliance with the Franks; his fleets meanwhile swept the seas, carrying the terror of the
dread Menapian's name to the remotest shores of
western Europe. At length Carausius was basely
assassinated by his prime minister, Allectus.

The types of the coins of Carausius are numerous; in the last edition of Mr. Akerman's
Coins of the Romans relating to Britain fifty-
three varieties in gold and silver are enumerated,
and no less than 233 in brass. Coins bearing
the portrait of Carausius are often found in the
neighbourhood of Richborough, in Kent, where
the Roman station of Rutupiæ formerly stood, off
which the Romano-British fleet was wont to ride
at anchor. Carausius's coins are also frequently
dredged up from the bed of the Thames, found
at St. Albans, *Verulamium*, or at other Roman
stations in the south of England; yet, notwithstanding the numbers and variety of the coinage
of the usurper, the coin found on the site of
Uriconium is unique. We give a representation

of this valuable and interesting specimen. "It is in brass, of the third size. The obverse pre-

sents the usual title of the emperor, but with the singular novelty of a bare and full-faced portrait. In both these respects it is unique, as all the coins of Carausius hitherto known, whether in gold, silver, or brass, present the portrait in profile, and either helmeted, laureated, or (as generally) with a radiated crown, but never bare. The work is good and the condition fine; the portrait as usual, bold and characteristic. The reverse is one of the most ordinary occurrence.

Obv.—IMP.CARAVSIVS.P.F.AVG. The bare head of Carausius, full-faced.

Rev.—SALVS AVG. An erect figure of a female (Hygeia), feeding out of a patera a serpent, which rises from the base of an altar. In the exergue the letter C, probably for *Clausentum*."[1]

[1] Extract from a paper by JOHN D. BERGNE, read before the Numismatic Society, Nov. 27, 1851, relative to a "Coin of Carausius, of a new and unpublished type"; the coin in question. *Numis. Chron.*, vol. xiv., p. 150, *et supra*.

The following description has been given by Mr. Roach Smith of the 132 coins described in page 23, as having been found with the skeleton of the old man in the hypocaust:—

LIST OF COINS

(CHIEFLY IN SMALL BRASS),

FOUND WITH THE SKELETONS IN THE HYPOCAUST AT WROXETER.

TETRICUS.

One of the *Fides Militum* type; much worn.

CLAUDIUS GOTHICUS.

Rer.—CONSECRATIIS. An eagle.

CONSTANTINVS MAXIMVS.

Obr.—CONSTANTINVS . MAX . AVG. Diademed or wreathed head to the right.

Rec.—GLORIA EXERCITVS. Two soldiers; between them two standards, or (in three instances) a single standard.

Mint marks.[1]—P. CONST., 3; TR.P, 6; SL.C., 1; illegible, 3.   Total, 13.

---

[1] Exergual letters.

CONSTANS.

Rev.—FEL . TEMP . REPARATIO. The emperor
standing in a galley, rowed by a Victory.
(Much worn.)

CONSTANTINVS II.

Obv.—CONSTANTINVS . IVN . NOB . C. Head
to the right, laureated; bust in armour.

Rev.—GLORIA EXERCITVS. Two soldiers
standing; between them two standards.

Mint marks.—TR . P. or TR . S., 15; P . E . C., 9;
CONST., 3; illegible, 9.

CONSTANTIVS II.

Obv.—FL . IVL . CONSTANTIVS . NOB . C. Laureated head to the right; bust in armour.

Rev.—GLORIA EXERCITVS. Two soldiers and
standards.

Mint marks.—TR . S., 3; D., 1; SMTST., 1.

Total, 5.

JULIANVS.

A plated Denarius.

Obv.—FL . CL . IVLIANVS . P . P . AUG. Diademed head to the right.

Rev.—VOTIS X . MVLT . XX., within a wreath.

HELENA.

Obr.—FL . IVL . HELENAE (*sic*) AVG. Head
to the right.

Rer.—PAX PVBLICA. A female figure standing,
holding in the right hand a branch; in
the left, a *hasta pura;* in the field, a
cross ✠. In exergue, TR . P.

Another, without the ✠. Total, 2.

THEODORA.

Obr.—FL . MAX . THEODORAE AVG. Head
to the right.

Rer.—PIETAS ROMANA. A female standing,
suckling an infant. In the exergue,
TRP.

VRBS ROMA.

The usual type.

Mint marks.—PL . C., 11 ; TR . P. or TR . S., 10;
illegible, 3. Total, 24.

CONSTANTINOPOLIS.

The usual types.

Mint marks.—TR . P., 20; P . L . C. or S . L . C., 9;
O . SIS., 1; S . CONST , 1; illegible, 3.
Total, 34.

VALENS.

Obr.—D . N . VALENS . . . . .

Rev.—SECVRITAS . . . . . . Victory, with wreath
and palm branch, marching to the left.
Much corroded.

Rude copies of some of the foregoing coins . 6
Extremely corroded 6

Tetricus	. 1
Claudius Gothicus . .	. 1
Constantinus I. . . .	. 13
Constans	. 1
Constantinus II. . .	. 36
Constantius II. . . .	. 5
Julianus	. 1
Helena	. 2
Theodora	. 1
Urbs Roma . . .	. 24
Constantinopolis . .	. 34
Valens	. 1
Barbarous copies (*Minimi*) .	. 6
Corroded and illegible .	. 6

Total number . . . 132

The smaller heap of thirty-eight coins, dropped apparently by some one as he was making his escape from the supposed enameller's shop, consisted of the following :—

Caracalla (a silver Denarius)	1
Severus Aloxander (a plated Denarius)	1
Maximus (second brass)	1
Gallienus	2
Salonina (copper, washed with silver).	1
Postumus	1
Victorinus	8
Tetricus	3
Claudius Gothicus	2
Carausius	1
The Constantine Family	12
Valentinian	1
Gratian (A.D. 375 to 383)	1
A *Minimus*	1
Decomposed	2
Total	38

Now, the discovery of these series of coins has a two-fold significance. In the first place, it shows what was the current money at the time in Britain ; secondly, and more important still, it presents us, it may be, with a clue to the date of the destruction of Uriconium, for it was in the year 383 that Magnus Maximus, assuming the imperial purple, according to Gildas, withdrew the garrisons and the flower of the British youth from Roman Britain, and left the enervated conquered population of this country at the mercy of their more hardy highland brethren.

Commenting on the catalogue of coins found with the old skeleton in the hypocaust, the eminent numismatist, who drew it up, observes— " The two earliest (chronologically), those of Tetricus and Claudius Gothicus, and the latest, that of Valens, are much worn from circulation; and the coin of Constans is in much the same state. But the others, and they are all of the Constantine family, are comparatively fresh, and bear no marks of having been worn much, if at all, by traffic.

" The worn condition of the coin of Valens indicates that the catastrophe which hastened the death of the three persons in the hypocaust, and probably destroyed the town, took place at some period during the reign of Valens, or a little subsequent to it. Now, it was in this very reign that Theodosius was sent into Britain, to check the inroads of the Saxons and Picts, as well as to put down what appears to have been an internal insurrection ;[1] and it is extremely probable that Uriconium may have been one of the towns which

---

[1] See *Ammianus Marcellinus*, lib. xxvii. xxviii.

I

had ere his arrival been partially overthrown, and which was then restored by Theodosius."[1] Or Uriconium may not have been restored by the Roman general, but remained, from the day on which the barbarians overthrew it till now, a mass of ruins. Against this latter supposition, however, we must place those *minimi* that were found. This interesting description of coinage apparently was a very rude imitation of the types of the Constantine family, yet as the *minimi* are unlike the Anglo-Saxon coinage, these are supposed to have been struck by the towns of Britain after the withdrawal of the Roman government, but previously to the establishment of the Anglo-Saxon kingdoms.

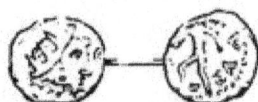

Subjoined is a representation of one of the *minimi* found at Uriconium.

A comparison of the coins mentioned in the foregoing lists points to the very latest period previous to the establishment of the Anglo-Saxons.

But there is a mystery hanging over the fate of Uriconium; and whether it was destroyed by the Picts, Scots, the ferocious Attacots, by some irruption of the original British population of

[1] *Numismatic Chronicle*, vol. xx., p. 79, *et seq.*

North Wales, or by some predatory band of roving Saxons, is unknown.

From its being mentioned, at the close of the seventh century, in the Chorography of Ravenna, as the chief city of the Cornavii, Baxter supposes that Uriconium flourished till the time of the Danes, and that perhaps even here, at one period, the Mercians fixed their capital. No Saxon coins, however, were found during the late excavations.

"I have seen, and had passing through my hands," says a well-informed numismatist,[1] "some thousands of the coins found at Uriconium; they are generally very much worn and defaced, and often found nearly oxydised by heat." Corroborative testimony that the city was destroyed by fire.

[1] Samuel Wood, Esq., F S A., of Shrewsbury.

CHAPTER XI.

THE CEMETERY.

IN every age mankind have recognised it as a
sacred duty to bury the dead. In the disposal
of the dead two methods prevailed among the
ancients:—1st, the burial of the entire body;
2ndly, the burial of the ashes after the body had
been burned. With respect to the former,
namely, the burial of the entire body, the manner
has varied; sometimes the body was inhumed,
that is, interred in the earth, as in all probability
the body of Abel, the first man who died, was
buried, and as the patriarch Jacob certainly
buried Rachel his wife, on the way to Ephrath,
setting a pillar upon her grave.[1] Sometimes
the body was placed in a cavern, as Abraham
buried Sarah in the cave of Machpelah;[2] or
the body was placed entire in a coffin, or sarco-
phagus, according to the manner of the ancient
Egyptians.

To prove that burning the dead was a very
ancient custom, we need only refer to Homer's
description of the magnificent funeral obsequies

---

[1] Gen. xxxv. 19-20.　　　[2] Ibid. xxiii. 19.

attending the burning of the bodies of Patroclus by the Greeks, and Hector by the Trojans.[1]

The Greeks and Romans, the latter of whom borrowed most of their funeral rites from the former, were especially solicitous about the interment of their deceased friends, since they were persuaded that until the body obtained sepulture the soul was excluded from the Elysian fields. With the Romans, the interment of the entire body in the ground appears to have been the most ancient method of disposing of the dead. Cicero[2] and Pliny[3] assert that burning, or cremation, was not practised until the time of Sylla, the Dictator; yet the law of the ancient code known as the XII. Tables, which enjoins that no body should be buried or burned within the city, implied that burning was sometimes practised by the Romans at a much earlier period. As the depositing the entire body in the ground was their first, so also it was the latest method adopted by the Romans in disposing of the dead; and the custom of burning, in all probability, went gradually out of use, as the doctrine of the resurrection of the body spread with the diffusion of Christianity.

Remains were found at Uriconium indicating that both modes of disposal of the dead just

---

[1] *Iliad*, bb. xxiii, xxiv.   [2] *De Legg.*, lib. ii., c. 22.
[3] *Hist. Nat.*, lib. vii., c. 54.

described had been practised by our Romano-
British forefathers resident at this town; the
practice of burning the dead, however, appears
to have predominated.

When a corpse was to be burnt, a pyramidic
pyra of rough inflammable pine wood, varying in
height according to the rank of the deceased, was
constructed. This was interspersed with shrubs,
when the body, sometimes wrapped in an incom-
bustible cloth called asbestos, having been placed
upon it, with averted faces, a token of unwilling
ministration, the nearest relatives applied the
torch to the pile. Perfumes and libatory offer-
ings, as well as objects that had belonged to
the deceased, were often thrown into the flames
of the roaring and crackling pile. The usual
ceremonies being completed, and the pile consumed, the bones and ashes of the deceased were
carefully collected and placed in an urn. Sepulchral urns varied in quality and make, according
to the taste and wealth of the friends of the
deceased; some funeral urns were costly, being
made of gold and silver; others were made of
bronze, marble, glass, or baked clay merely; and
sepulchral urns were inscribed or plain. It was
usual to deposit in the urn, along with the calcined bones and ashes, various articles, such
as a lachrymatory, or a lamp, and a coin; this
latter the heathen Romans supposed would be

required by the deceased, wherewith to pay his passage in Charon's boat across the dismal river Styx.

The Romans usually buried the dead without the walls of their cities by the highways—a sanatory precaution fearfully neglected in mediæval and in modern times. By thus committing the dust of those whom they had loved to earth by the roadside, the memory of the dead was prevented passing into oblivion, and the wayfarer was often reminded of his own mortality. The interesting Roman family vault, described in pages 14 and 15 as having been discovered in the year 1798 at Uriconium, was situated outside the city, and doubtless stood by the side of the ancient via that communicated between this town and the Roman station of Segontium. On account, however, of more numerous remains of a sepulchral character having been found outside the eastern gate of Uriconium, adjoining the Watling Street-road, it is the latter which more appropriately may be termed the "Street of the Tombs."

The cemetery of Uriconium probably extended along either side of the road which approached the eastern side of the city; there can be no doubt that it extended a considerable distance along the southern side of this Watling Street, since, in the field abutting this road on the south, many Roman sepulchral relics from time to time have been brought to light. It was here that in the year 1752 were found those three large Roman sepulchral stones which are now in the library of the Shrewsbury Grammar School, and in this field modern agricultural operations have frequently ploughed up fragments of broken urns. On September 16th, 1861, the workmen began to trench the so-called cemetery in every direction, and they found *wood ashes* in no less than a dozen different places. Here also they discovered the glass vases and glass lachrymatory engraved in *plate* XI., and described in pages 67 and 68. There were also fragments of other glass vessels found in the field alluded to, and likewise other lachrymatories, some of which were *half-melted;* from whence it would seem that these had been cast into the funereal flames. The lamp, with its maker's name, MODES, upon it, at the bottom, which is engraved in *plate* X., various specimens of Samian ware, and eighteen or nineteen cinerary urns, were picked up in the field. Many of the urns were broken, yet some were entire, and these contained burnt human bones. In one of the cinerary urns there was not only burnt bones and ashes found, but a lachrymatory also, and *a single copper coin.*

Only one portion of a building was found in the cemetery. It consisted of a few feet of rec-

tangular walls, eighteen inches thick, and not
descending deep into the ground; this may be
the remains of a sepulchral vault, or it may mark
the site of the *ustrinum*, or place set apart for
burning the dead. The position of the building
alluded to is indicated in *plate* I.; the dotted lines
represent what is conjectured to be the remains of
a street leading to the building.

The sepulchral urns found in the neighbourhood of Wroxeter appear to have been simply
buried in the earth, without any protecting chest
or tomb; but there is a sepulchral urn, preserved
in the Shrewsbury Museum, that came from the
cemetery of Uriconium, which is enclosed in a
leaden case. No stone sepulchral chests, such
as that remarkable one found at Avisford,[1] or

---

[1] The Roman chest, or tomb, alluded to was found at Avisford,
in Sussex, in the year 1817. Upon the removal of about nine
inches of superincumbent soil, a neat flat stone was discovered
covering a coffin, five feet long, two feet wide, and fifteen inches
deep. In this chest there had never been an entire corpse, for
within the coffin, in its centre, stood a beautiful large square
green glass vase, with a reeded handle, in which were calcined
bones. Around the bottle, or vase, were ranged numerous
vessels and articles used in ancient sepulture, namely, "three
elegantly-shaped earthen vases with handles; several paterae; a
pair of sandals studded with innumerable little hexagonal brass
nails, fancifully arranged; three lamps; four slipper boats (lamp
stands), placed at the four corners on brackets, or corbels; an
oval dish and handle, escalloped round the edge, containing a
transparent agate, the shape and size of a pigeon's egg," etc.
A representation of the interior of this remarkable sepulchral
chest, and the various objects as they were discovered standing
in it, is given in vol. i. *plate* xliv., *Collect. Antiqua.*

sarcophagi, such as those interesting carved and inscribed ones, which were found in the neighbourhood of York (*Eburacum*[1]), have hitherto been discovered at Uriconium.

There was found, however, on the 18th of September, 1861, in the cemetery of Uriconium, the fragment of a large tomb that appears to have been surmounted by a statue, of which the feet only remain. On one side of this stone there is a Latin inscription, contained in seven lines, which has hitherto baffled antiquarian ingenuity

to make out. The annexed woodcut represents the monument in question, the slab of which is supposed to bear the following inscription; but many of the letters, and particularly those in the lowermost lines, are doubtful, owing to the damage which the stone unfortunately has sustained :—

---

[1] Engraved in *plates* xi. and xii. of the Rev. C. WELL-BELOVED's learned work on *Eburacum, or York, under the Romans.*

123

AMINIVS . T . POL . F . A
NORVMXXXXVSTIPXXII . MIL . LEG.
IIGEM . MILITAVITAQNVNC IIIC SII
LEGITE . ET . FELICES . VITA . FLVS . MINV
IVSTAVINIERAQVATIEGIIIE . INTV
TANARA . DITIS . VIVITE . DVMSPI . . .
VITAE . DAT . TEMPVS . HONESTE.[1]

The three first lines of this curious inscription,
apparently, may be rendered as follows :—

Aminius (or Flaminius), *Titi Pollioni Filius*,
annorum XXXXV., *Stipendiorum* XXII. miles *legionis*
VII. geminæ. Militavit *aquilifer.* Nunc hic *situs est.*

The subjoined represent two out of the three
sepulchral stones, mentioned in pages 14 and 15,
as having been found in the year 1752, and as
being now preserved in the library of the
Grammar School at Shrewsbury. These were
found accidentally by men employed in digging a
drain on the side of the pretty bank that over-
hangs the south side of the Watling Street-road.
From this eminence a lovely view may be obtained ; it was the site of the ancient cemetery of
Uriconium. We are informed that figs. 1 and 2
had been fastened by tenons into mortices cut

---

[1] It has been suggested by Dr. M'Caul, of Toronto, in his
work on *Britanno-Romano Inscriptions*, that the latter portion
of this inscription, which evidently contains three lines in hexa-
meter verse, may be—

Perlegite et felices vitâ plus minus jutâ ;
Omnibus æqua lege iter est ad Taenara Ditis.
Vivite, dum Stygius vitæ dat tempus honeste.

Like the above, however, it is merely a conjectural reading.

into other stones that lay flat within, and that
they had been buried into the ground, as our

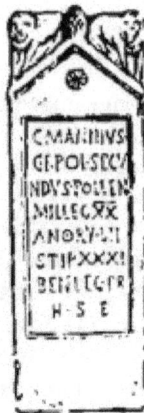

modern tombstones are, up to the tablets containing the inscriptions.

The stone represented on the left bears the
following inscription :—

C. MANNIVS   Caius Mannius,
C. F. POL. SECV   Caii filius, Pollia, Secu
NDVS. POLLEN   ndus, Pollentia,
MIL. LEG. XX   miles legionis XX.,
ANORV. LII   annorum LII.,
STIP. XXXI   stipendiorum XXXI.,
BEN. LEG. PR   beneficiarius legati principalis,
H. S. E.   hic situs est.

Of this, the translation appears to be:—"Caius
Mannius Secundus, son of Caius, of the Pollian
tribe, of Pollentia, a soldier of the twentieth
legion, fifty-two years of age, having served
thirty-one years, a beneficiary of the principal
legate, lies here."

The twentieth legion had its head-quarters at
Deva, Chester, distant about fifty miles from
Uriconium.

Upon the sepulchral tablet, represented to the
right on page 124, are inscribed these lines:—

M . PETRONIVS	*Marcus* Petronius,
L . F . MEN	*Lucii filius Menenia,*
VIC . ANN	*vicsit annis*
XXXVIII	XXXVIII.,
MIL . LEG	*miles legionis*
XIIII . GEM	XIIII *gominæ,*
MILITAVIT	*militavit*
ANN . XVIII	*annis* XVIII.,
SIGN . FVIT	*signifer fuit.*
H . S . E.	*hic situs est.*

It may be translated thus:—"Marcus Petronius,
son of Lucius, of the Menenian tribe, lived thirty-
eight years, a soldier of the fourteenth legion,
called Gemina; he served as a soldier eighteen
years, and was a standard-bearer. He lies
here."

"A friend, who has paid some attention to

the history of the fourteenth legion," writes
Mr. Scarth, "and who is familiar with this inscription, says — 'I feel certain that Petronius
was a bearer of one of the signa of the fourteenth legion in the famous victory over Boadicea,
A.D. 61. This legion arrived in Britain A.D. 43,
when Petronius, being only twenty years old,
was a *miles gregarius*, and subsequently, for his
valour, perhaps, under Ostorius Scapula, raised to
the rank of Signifer. Being only thirty-eight
when he died, the year of his death was probably
A.D. 62. It could not have been much later, for
in A.D. 68, the fourteenth legion was quartered in
Dalmatia (Tacitus). He may have died in consequence of his wounds in the year 61. At any
rate, this inscription is very interesting.'"[1] As it
has been well observed, however, by Mr. Wright,
"Surely the fact of a soldier having been buried
in a certain locality is not alone a proof that the
whole legion, to which he belonged, was there
with him"; and "as the fourteenth legion was
long stationed in Germany, Marcus Petronius
may have come thence on a visit to Britain, and
died at Uriconium, at a much later date than that
to which this monument is supposed to belong."[2]
The sepulchral stones referred to are about six
feet in length.

[1] *Archæological Journal*, vol. xvi., pp. 63—64.
[2] *Journal of the Brit. Arch. Assoc.* for 1859, p. 207.

Of the two monuments represented below, the
one to tho left is the third of the sepulchral

stones described as having been found in the
cemetery of Uriconium in 1752. As will be seen
from the engraving, this stone is divided into
three compartments, the inscription in the first
of which appears to be as follows :—

D . M	*Diis Manibus.*
PLACIDA	*Placida,*
AN . LV	*annorum LV.,*
CVR . AG	*curam agente*
CONI . A	*conjuge annorum*
XXX.	XXX.

The translation is -- "To the gods of the
Shades. Placida, aged fifty-five; raised by the
care of her husband, who had been her husband
thirty years."

128

The inscription on the second column is—

D . M	*Diis Manibus.*
DEVCCV	*Douccu*
S . AN . XV	*e, annorum XV.,*
CVR . AG	*curam agente*
RATRE.	*fratre.*

Namely, "To the gods of the Shades, Douccus, aged fifteen years; raised by the care of his brother."

The third compartment of the interesting sepulchral stone alluded to is left blank, as if for the reception of the husband and father's name, when he, it may be, should return from duty in some distant land, and be laid beside his family. Meanwhile, to fraternal, rather than paternal love, it seems had been entrusted the burial of poor Douccus.

A fourth Roman monumental stone is preserved in the library of the Shrewsbury Grammar School; this, which is more mutilated than the others, also came from the cemetery of Uriconium, where it was found in the year 1810. From it was sketched the tablet represented on the right of page 127. Above there is executed a rude bas-relief of a horseman riding over a falling figure, beneath which is the following :—

TIB . CLAVD . TER	*Tiberius Claudius Tere*
NTIVS . EQ . COH	*ntius, eques cohortis*
THRACVM . AN	*Thracum, ann*
ORVM . LVII . STIP	*orum LVII., stip*
ENDIORVM	*endiorum . . . . .,*
H . S.	*hic situs est.*

Namely, "Tiberius Claudius Terentius, a horseman of the cohort of Thracians, aged fifty-seven
years, having served . . . . . lies here."

The tombstone of a horseman of this same body
of Thracians has been found at Cirencester, the
site of the Roman town of Corinium. Had the
cohort of Thracian cavalry originally belonged
to Uriconium, and afterwards been stationed at
Corinium, we do not know. Yet this inscription
proves the fact, that of the soldiery employed by
Rome to garrison Britain all were not Roman in
their origin; and other races, besides the pure
Italian, had a hand in the subjugation of our
country. The valuable record, entitled the *Notitia*,
the authenticity of which is undisputed, and which
must have been drawn up before the Roman
troops left Britain, gives a list of the various
auxiliary troops then (that is, towards the close
of the Roman domination) on active duty along
the south-eastern, eastern, and northern coasts of
Britain; from whence we learn that Spaniards,
Gauls, Germans, Dalmatians, Cilicians, Moors,
Dacians, Tungrians, etc., as well as Thracians,
assisted to hold Britain at the foot of old Rome.
The same record informs us that the twenty-sixth
cohort of Britons was stationed in Armenia, that
a troop of the "Invincible Younger Britons"
was serving in Spain, and the fourth ala of
Britons in Egypt. Thus served British youth in

K

many other parts of the Roman Empire. Thus did politic Rome of old destroy, by amalgamating them, the nationalities she had trampled down; when drawing upon the resources of the various countries her might had vanquished, she made their manhood subserve her grand purpose of Universal Empire. Do it observed, however, that the various foreign auxiliaries sent by Rome to garrison her strongholds in Britain used the Latin language; in short, relinquishing their own nationalities, they became, to all intents and purposes, Roman.

The remains of at least twenty different skeletons were dug up in an orchard opposite Wroxeter Church, to the right of the Watling Street Road, as it runs down to the river. The circumstances under which these skeletons were found are interesting. The bodies had not been thrown heedlessly into a pit, but appeared to have been carefully buried, for the skeletons lay at full length, generally near to each other, with legs and arms extended, or with one arm lying across the body. No vestiges of wood, weapons, articles of domestic use, or apparel, were found. Of the nineteen crania dug up, no less than eleven were more or less crooked; a peculiarity which gave rise to much discussion, many being of opinion that the persons to whom these skulls had belonged lived and died with deformed heads. As

Dr. Henry Johnson, however, has pointed out, "there can be little doubt that the deformity has been produced by posthumous pressure, aided by moisture and the solvent action of certain acids that always exist in vegetable mould."[1] It is doubtful whether these had been Roman remains.

The discovery is recorded of the finding, on the site of Uriconium, at a former period, the altar-like stone, represented on the left of the two sketches subjoined. The stone in question appears

to have been formed, during the middle ages, into a holy-water stoop. Upon its side the following Roman inscription may be read :—

BONA REIPVBLICÆ NATVS.

During the course of the late exploration the fragment represented above, to the right, was found. The letters read D. M.; underneath which, apparently, can be traced ISVM. The

[1] See *Abstract of Proceedings of Royal Society*, June, 1862.

D. M. may indicate a tombstone; or taken in connection with the inscription underneath, it is possible that, in this instance, these letters may stand for *deo maximo*, and so this fragment may have belonged to an altar dedicated to Jupiter, *Joel SVMmo.*

Although sepulchral remains and monuments, bearing, like these, the marks of heathenism stamped upon them, have from time to time been discovered on the site of Uriconium, there has been no inscription or other relic found here appearing to have the most remote allusion to Christianity. Nor, if we are to trust antiquarians, have any traces of Christianity been found among the innumerable Roman remains found in this country, notwithstanding these embrace many altars and inscriptions of temples to the false gods. But was it not, some one may ask, when under the government of the Romans, that the first rays of the light of Christianity shone upon our beloved country?

In an enquiry relating to the introduction of Christianity into Britain, it should be remembered that until the time of Constantine the Great, A.D. 306—337, the Roman was a Pagan state, and, with but few exceptions, its Cæsars, emperors, and governors persecuted the followers of Christianity in every part of the empire. This, in some degree, may account for the scarcity

of British public Christian memorials of the
Roman period. It may be added, that the existence of vital Christianity in a country is not
incompatible with the total absence of stone or
bronze memorials.

There is reason to believe that the glad tidings
of salvation were heard by Romano-British ears;
yet who first preached the gospel, or was the
honoured instrument of planting a Christian
Church in this island, will in all probability
never be known. Deeply interesting as this
subject is, it is involved in great obscurity.

To St. John, St. James the Great, St. James
the Less, Simon Zelotes, to St. Peter, Joseph of
Arimathea, St. Paul,[1] and to that Aristobulus of
whom St. Paul speaks,[2] as well as to many others,
has been ascribed the distinction of having first
brought the knowledge of Christ into Britain;
yet of all the various individuals to whom tradition has assigned the heavenly undertaking,
the claim of the great Apostle to the Gentiles is
supported by the most ancient and venerable
authorities.

The second landing of the Romans in Britain

---

[1] In his Epistle to the Colossians, chap. I., ver. 23, the Apostle
Paul, speaking of the gospel, makes use of this strong expression—"which was preached to every creature which is under
heaven." Clemens Romanus, the fellow-labourer of St. Paul,
represents this apostle as preaching the gospel to the utmost
bounds of the west.

[2] Romans xvi. 10.

occurred A.D. 43, or about ten years after the crucifixion of our Lord. There is no doubt that the Christian religion had gained a footing in Rome, and even engaged the attention of the government, previously to the death of the Emperor Claudius, A.D. 54. *Camulodunum*, Colchester, and *Verulamiam*, St. Albans, had become flourishing *municipiæ*, or free cities, before the revolt of Boadicea; and London, although not yet honoured with the name of a colony, was considerable, from the resort of merchants, and from its maritime trade.[1] Under such circumstances, it is not too much to presume that there was a constant and even daily military and commercial communication between Rome and this its province. Many Britons of high rank, also, having been carried captive to Rome, and others, going thither with followers, to negotiate their affairs at the Imperial Court, combined to render it unlikely that anything which made a noise at Rome could long remain unknown in this island.

Among the great number of persons who came from Rome into Britain, to occupy civil and military posts, was Aulus Plautius, the very first Roman to whom was entrusted the government of Britain. Concerning the lady of Aulus Plautius, Tacitus gives the following account:—

---

[1] TACITUS, *Ann*, lib. xiv., c. 33.

"Pomponia Gracina, a lady of distinction, married to Plautius, who was honoured with an ovation for his victories in Britain, was accused of having embraced a foreign superstition, and her trial for that crime was committed to her husband. Plautius assembled her kindred, and in observance of ancient law and custom, having in their presence held solemn inquisition upon the conduct and character of his wife, pronounced her innocent of anything immoral." [1] Lipsius and others are of opinion that what is here called "a foreign superstition" was the Christian religion. If this illustrious lady was really a Christian, and accompanied her husband during his residence in Britain, from A.D. 43 to A.D. 47, she might not only have taught it to her household, but engaged others to preach the gospel in Britain at a very early period.

In St. Paul's 2nd epistle to Timothy, chap. iv., ver. 21, we find this passage :—"Eubulus greeteth thee, and *Pudens*, and Linus, and *Claudia*, and all the brethren." It is believed that the Pudens here mentioned was a Roman of exalted birth, and Claudia a British princess, daughter of Cogidunus, the client king of the Emperor Claudius, in honour of whom the daughter had been named Claudia. Cogidunus reigned over

---

[1] TACITUS, *Annal.*, lib. xiii., c. 32.

tho Regni, who inhabited Sussex and the greater part of Surrey; Chichester was his capital.

Now the poet Martial, in one of his epigrams, writes—

> "Claudia, Rufe, meo nubit Peregrina Pudenti ;
> Macte esto tædis O Hymenæe tuis ! etc.
> > lib. iv., epi. 13.

Claudia Peregrina, Rufus, is about to be married to my friend Pudens. Be propitious, Hymen, with thy torches !"

And again—

> "Claudia cæruleis quam sit Rufina Britannis,
> Edita quam Latiæ pectora plebis habet !
> Quale decus formæ ! Romanam credere matres
> Italides possunt, etc.
> > lib. xi., epi. 53.

Although born among the blue-eyed Britons, how folly has Claudia Rufina the intelligence of the Roman people ! What beauty is hers ! The matrons of Italy might take her for a Roman," etc.

In such strains of admiration did the celebrated heathen epigrammist write concerning that British lady whom his friend Pudens married. There is little doubt that the Pudens and Claudia, of whom Martial wrote, are the Pudens and Claudia alluded to by St. Paul in his epistle. In the latter epigram quoted Pudens is called Holy — *Sanctus Maritus;* a strong presumption that he was one of those who were esteemed such, or, in other words, that Pudens was a Christian. It is not improbable that along with his distinguished wife

Pudens may have come over into Britain, when
taking up their abode at Chichester, here these
bosom friends of the apostle may have taught the
cause that lay nearest to his heart.

According to the undoubtedly very ancient
British Triads,[1] it was Bran, a British prince,
the father of Caradog, or Caractacus, that brought
the faith first into this island. The British chief
Caractacus having been betrayed, was sent a
prisoner with his family, including, it is said, his
father, to Rome, as hostages, where they remained
several years, A.D. 51—58. During this interval
the tradition is that they were converted under
the teaching of the Apostle Paul, and returning
to their native land, Bran is said to have become
a very zealous and successful propagator of
Christianity. Hence we read in the 18th Triad
concerning "The Three Holy Families of Britain :
—1. The *first*, the family of *Bran the Blessed* up
Llyr Llediaith ; that Bran brought the faith in
Christ first into this island from Rome " This
assertion is repeated in Triad 35, relating to
" The Three Sovereigns of the Isle of Britain
who conferred blessings :—1. Bran the Blessed,
who first brought the faith of Christ to the

---

[1] The claims of this very ancient species of bardic and
Druidic lore to genuineness have been disputed, yet not by
Welsh scholars. For a very able vindication of the ancient
British poems, the reader is referred to SHARON TURNER'S
History of the Anglo-Saxons, vol. iii., p. 449, et seq., 7th edit.

Cymry from Rome, where he had been a hostage for his son Carudog seven years."

Tertullian, who flourished in the latter half of the second century, has left on record the following remarkable words: — "*et Britannorum inaccessa Romanis loca, Christo vero subdita;*[1] and those parts of Britain which were inaccessible to the Romans, are become subject to Christ."

Origen, who flourished A.D. 220, in his fourth Homily on Ezekiel, bears similar decisive testimony to the antiquity of the British Church, for "when," asks he, "before the advent of Christ did the land of Britain agree in the worship of one God? *quando enim terra Britanniæ ante adventum Christi, in unius Dei consensit religionem?*"

St. Athanasius, who wrote A.D. 350, alluding to his trial before the Council of Sardis, at which there were more than 300 bishops present, states most distinctly that bishops came from the British territories; from whence may be inferred not only that there was in the British isles a Christian Church in full organization, but that its bishops were of sufficient consequence to be cited to this grand council.

Eusebius, A.D. 270—340; Arnobius, A.D. 306; Jerome, A.D. 329—420; Chrysostom, A.D. 400;

---

[1] TERTUL. *Adv. Judæ*, c. 7.

and Theodoret, A.D. 423, all give evidence tending to show that Christianity had been introduced into Britain previous to the withdrawal of the Romans.

We say nothing concerning the attendance of British bishops at the council held at Arles, in Gaul, in the year 314; or about their presence at the council summoned by Constantius to Ariminum in Italy, A.D. 359, supported, nevertheless, as assertions to that effect are, by evidence of a substantial character. Those ecclesiastical meetings which Bede, Nennius, and the later chroniclers, who, building upon their narratives, or upon still more ancient tradition, affirm were held at *Verulamium*, St. Albans, and other places in Britain, we also pass over, because the most ancient notices relating to these alleged British councils are contained in works penned after the events alluded to are said to have taken place. Of the former authorities quoted, however, all of them wrote *before* the Romans finally abandoned Britain, say A.D. 440. The authors of those works, upon the authority of which we base our reasoning concerning the very early introduction of Christianity into Britain, were dead and in their graves, many of them hundreds of years, the latest of them at least 150 years, before the coming of St. Augustine. Austin, or Augustine, landed upon the Isle of Thanet in the year 597.

It is clear, therefore, that he could not have first
introduced Christianity into Britain. This mis-
sionary from Rome brought Christianity to our
pagan Anglo-Saxon forefathers, we grant; but a
British Church appears to have flourished centuries ere good Pope Gregory's Italian mission
was dreamt of. Every schoolboy has heard of
St. Augustino's famous interview with the clergy
of the British Church,[1] in order to induce them
to acknowledge the bishop of Rome as their
chief, and to celebrate Easter at the same time as
the Church of Rome did. To these, and other
propositions of a similar import, the British eccle-
siastics firmly refused to assent, telling the Italian,
at the same time, that they acknowledged as their
spiritual overseer the Bishop of Caerleon-on-Usk.
Can anything show more distinctly than this does
the antiquity and independence of the British
Church?

Nor should it be forgotten that there were in
Ireland, and in Scotland also, in the fifth and
sixth centuries, Christian schools famous for their
learning; and athwart a surrounding darkness
and barbarism bright rays of Christian light
shot far and wide from the renowned seminary of
St. Finian, at Clonard, near the Boyne, and from
the Isle of Hy, or Iona, in the Hebrides.

[1] They met at a place called Aust-cliffe, in Gloucestershire,
near the usual ferry over the Severn into Wales.

To sum the whole matter up, we believe that there were in Britain native converts to the faith before the end of the first century; our most ancient historian, Gildas, is probably not far from the truth when he speaks of Christianity having been introduced into Britain about the time of the revolt of Boadicea, A.D. 60.

Yet, notwithstanding the evidence in favour of the Christian religion having been introduced at a very early period into Britain, not a trace of it has been found among the innumerable religious and sepulchral monuments belonging to the Roman period; a circumstance so remarkable as to have led some learned men to doubt even whether Christianity had any existence in Roman Britain. The most ancient Christian relics in this country are said to be some sepulchral stones found in Cornwall and Wales, usually assigned to the fifth and sixth centuries. These have crosses at their tops, and they bear names, evidently Celtic, amid inscriptions written in a corrupt Latin, not across the stone, as Roman inscriptions run, but incised lengthways.

We repeat, no sepulchral stone of a Christian character was found in the cemetery of Uriconium; and this it is which has led us into a somewhat long digression, to show, it by no means follows that here may not sleep humble disciples of Jesus. If the ashes of some who of old believed in

Christ rest by any of the waysides hereabouts, then instead of Gorgon's head, with snaky hairs, being carved over their tomb—dread symbol of a heathenism which afforded no hope!—in reference to their memory the apostle's exclamation of rapturous delight might more appropriately have been used—"O death, where is thy sting? O grave, where is thy victory? The sting of death is sin; and the strength of sin is the law. But thanks be to God, which giveth us the victory through our Lord Jesus Christ."

CHAPTER XII.

CONCLUSION.

LEAVE we the fields where the ashes of the legionary and proconsul miugling, await the summons of the archangel!

Let us retrace our footsteps to the ruined city, and, ere bidding it farewell, ascend the mound of debris thrown up by the excavators during their recent labours, as from thence one can obtain a fine view of the surrounding scenery. Upon that mountain, distant some ten miles off towards the south-west, the British prince Caractacus is said to have made his last stand against the Roman invader, ere Cartismandua basely betrayed him. Called Caer-Caradoc, or Caradog, which in the Welsh tongue signifies the fortress of Caractacus, the hill alluded to, accordingly, has ever since been traditionally associated with that hero's exploits. The leal-hearted Cymrian fell, and his conqueror built Uriconium, which in its turn has fallen, and now we contemplate its ruins.

Here, then, let us pause to reflect upon all that may be learnt from a survey of these dismantled walls, and the relics recovered from their midst; for by comparing the remains dug up from the

site of Uriconium, wo may obtain a very great
insight into the condition of the inhabitants of
Roman Britain. We learn their manners and
customs. By these remains wa aro taught that
during the Roman era our country was peopled
by various races, who made use of the Latin
language. All fragmentary although the relics
from this provincial town of the past are, they
serve as data, whence we may arrive at a more
accurate judgment respecting the state of the
arts, and trade, and manufacture at that period
in this country. They show us, moreover, that
our ancient forefathers enjoyed the comforts, and
even luxuries of life, in a far greater measure
than is generally supposed.

Amid all these evidences of civilisation, however, we find no recognition of God.

The city seems to have been surprised, and
fell; its destruction, in all probability, being accompanied by circumstances of peculiar horror.
Nor is Uriconium the only city in this country
which has ceased to exist, for a number of great
Roman towns are known to have once flourished
in Britain, the very sites of which are disputed
questions among the learned, so effectually have
these cities been expunged from the map. How
came it to pass that a centre of civilisation such
as this was blotted out? Nor need we, like a
Marius or Volney, go far off to find a fallen

145

greatness over which to moralise, as here, underneath neighbouring acres, lie buried the ruins
of a city.

The causes of the decline and fall of Rome
have been traced by an abler hand than mine, and
it has shown how luxury and licentiousness combined to lay, in the full meridian of empire, the
mightiest city the world e'er knew at the feet of
Alaric and the Vandals. The simplicity of a Cin-
cinnatus and the integrity of a Cato were gone, and
the noble Roman character had become sullied by
fearful profligacy. On the one hand was a nobility
degraded by vice and folly; on the other, an
ignorant populace, dangerously swaying to and
fro with frequent and capricious tumult. Then,
too, were seen in their full magnitude the evils of
a disputed succession, and the disorders con-
sequent on military despotism.

Drunk with the blood of saints, whose mangled
limbs had bestrewn her amphitheatre and places
of amusement—the cup of iniquity full! Rome
tottered and fell; when into the vortex of destruction was drawn Uriconium, for there is
little doubt that to the withdrawal of the Roman
legions from Britain the downfall of this city
may be indirectly traced.

Manifold as were the advantages which Britain
owed to the Roman domination, it cannot bo
denied that from this rich and fruitful province

L.

the Italian conquerors wrung an oppressive tribute. It is but too painfully certain, also, that along with civilisation they imparted their vices to the unfortunate Britons.

Unmanned by long submission to a foreign yoke, and its inhabitants enervated probably by luxury, Uriconium was unable to defend herself; her superior civilisation availed not, and in an evil hour some remorseless assailant put out her lamp.

Let not lessons taught by the history of our own country be lost upon us!

It is evening. The sun's glorious orb is sinking slowly behind the western mountains, and his setting rays are casting their golden beams over the landscape. Note the spires of village churches tipped as with living fire; watch how the distant hills gradually change hue, as the shadows of evening fast close around. The sunlight lingers on the summit of the lofty Wrekin, until at length the mountain seems a cold-looking vast mound. Twilight and its still quietude accords with the train of reflection into which the pilgrim-visitor to the ruins of the Roman city, it may be, has fallen. He figures to himself that great town, whose walls his eyes can just dimly discern, reno-vated in pristine splendour, with its terraced villas overhanging the Severn, and with its sculptured porticoes. Before him Roman veterans appear guarding the city gates; here a victorious legion

defiles past with rapid march. Sandalled Romano-
Britons, in tunic and in toga, stand talking in
the Forum and market-place of Uriconium, or
bending their steps onwards through its busy
streets. Yonder is the governor, with attendant
guard. He is engaged in a deep conversation
with some officer; their talk, it may be, is
concerning intelligence just arrived from the
capital, Rome: who likeliest to succeed in the
bloody struggle for the purple; Carausius's bold
revolt; or it may be news brought from Deva, or
Caerleon, which so absorbs their attention. That
sacrificial procession, headed by those sacerdotal
chiefs, wends its way to the neighbouring fane,
where Jupiter, chiefest of Rome's false gods, sits
glittering in profane splendour on a gilded throne.

Into a day-dream such as this the visitor, it
may be, has fallen, when starting from his
reverie he looks around, and sees through the
twilight nought but a mass of ruins—the fragments of a city once teeming with living and
throbbing humanity, but which has now been
numbered with the dead more than fourteen
hundred years. An awful interval! Compared
to it what an insignificant span does the life of
man seem! There the grey skeleton walls of the
lonely city stand naked and exposed, as if swept
with the besom of destruction.

FINIS.

INDEX.